"A"
13—21

By the same author

LOUIS ZUKOFSKY

"A"
13–21

JONATHAN CAPE
THIRTY BEDFORD SQUARE
LONDON

THIS COLLECTION FIRST PUBLISHED 1969
© 1969 BY LOUIS ZUKOFSKY

JONATHAN CAPE LTD
30 BEDFORD SQUARE, LONDON WCI

SBN 224 61500 9

My greetings and thanks for first appearances of:
"A"–20 to *Agenda* (London); "A"–13 and 16 to
Origin (Kyoto); "A"–14, 15, 17, 18, 19 and 21
(Prologue, Acts I, II, III) to *Poetry* (Chicago)
L. Z.

PRINTED IN GREAT BRITAIN
BY RICHARD CLAY (THE CHAUCER PRESS) LTD,
BUNGAY, SUFFOLK

CONTENTS

"A"
13–21

13

partita

What do you want to know
What do you want to do,
In a trice me the gist us;

Don't believe things turn untrue
A sea becomes teacher;
When the son takes his wife

Follows his genius,
Found in search
Come out of mysteries.

The husband who fights—
Doctors don't heal;
Watch out

Marriage is fast, wit
Less than fate
Look to love.

She'll have a son
And he honor, her heart desires
You let

Her correct you,
No one will hurt if
You can't count zeros.

Think of yourself, but honestly
The happiness to come
Delays his return.

A daughter has her mother's virtues
Everybody has enemies
The sick want company

Inheritances are not worth the hope
Losses recoup unexpected
The conqueror becomes powerless

Don't bet. Don't suppose,
Prove the foreigner;
Don't be touchy

You'll travel by sea
And land and air now
Justice doesn't see

To hear coins—
The paroled
Forgets his prison quickly.

Look at sky after
You cross your threshold,
Arrange your house before

You go, come back and find
The toys you had at one, two,
Three, four are

Dustless so that in littlest
Turns their great Creation, but not with
Your desire to be complete.

Meant to be seasonal;
Red pipecleaner velvet wired to
Valentine head with gold heart

Pledged you, the gift shop summer
Chip of night enamel horse.
Tiniest brass lock a little girl

Played with in her earliest
Fall, Japanese miniature guardians of
Home primary colored carved

Man and wife watch; music box
Coffee grinder handle loose in
Its child faery German scene.

For granite, the Egyptian
Hippopotamus; for days on days snow, tinsel
Spangled pincushion, pink

Flax basket stranded to yellow
Starred crosshatch by the ship
Sailing in a sealed bottle,

A paper weight a white bear
On a piece of rock, glass earrings
In the black snuff box

That was your father's mother's
Heirloom, its mate grandfather's
Walnut box with inlaid mother-of-pearl lid

One corner knifed near the wood hinge
As fleeing the Fire in silk white
Bonaparte's grenadier wished plunder in it

It did not have.
That that world was bitter
Was world—

The grace of a madhouse—courtesy, *Thanks
for passover delicacies
specially the black bambino*

11

(bambini plural) Aint tasted
that kind of ADmired chocolate
for 40 years—

Candy nigger babies and the beast Apartheider
Hind-dependence of gold dust Africa
On slaviest business, free root's old pest,

Not Nick in Ike nor Ike in Niké
Could Rhyme *love dove*—tale the
Stall in crew's chief, earth and

Daughter, please tell the clergyman
Your old man doesn't want any prayer
He has nothing to ask of *Him*.

I won't say that 'the world'
Grows more attaching—
The universe simply does;

The luxury, the magnificent waste
Of thought fed, fed, consecrated
Impingements on things, boundlessly

Personal relations (my own)
Their interminable numbers
Hope may well break before,

As I look at you today
And the trouble is
I am immortal facing

Four thousand eight hundred solar cells
Of four paddle wheels orbiting
Only one hundred sixty thousand years

To come down, burn up in
The earth's atmosphere somewhere around
Several hundred thousand miles "altitude" —

And this whole mountain of continent under
Iced Antarctica. Weed
Wandering jew growing

In two fingers of water in
Desk inkwell—a good thrust
For Bach's partita.

"Not fifty million miles to the sun?"
"Fifty thousand—enough?" Night, and
There is day,

And night is night
Day is day; that to this round
The missile from the fissile be weeded

Petulance envious of
A defense that collects junk
Sense a distaste among foes.

Offer as instrument
Avoid their rules like a disease
Don't bring on the judges

The Lame God's tripods
Themselves run to the Gods
Sings Who Wedded The Song

As shuttle weaves
Straightway plectrum pinks
Where is

The hirer
Where the help.
Not old at thirty

To rear the monument
Of your own fame on the slob—
If your children forget

Your love is not unregarded—
What is cold in the grave?
To rely solely on friendship

Is sad do not tax what holds
Back, branching from the wretched old
Expect bark to mix

Any color every sun
The second provides for itself.
Shave for a penny—THOTH.

Then politics hardly
Affect your fortune
Thieves do not rob

Health from old shoes
Parsimony does not beef
Poor faces, surety of

The high rope in the
Hinge of the knee
The farthest courses of the tent

Call you rich;
Wed—when wed
The generations be courteous.

Lost in the brakes sick
Tigers, a door sign
Mangling done here

To recover
Your coat don't
Lose your shirt, don't kick down

The ladder you stepped up
Your image in the eyes of
Her love, do not tell her

14

Your story by halves
He cabbages books
She twists the needle

These love and don't sleep.
The pleasure of reduced
Comfort are you sure

It was stolen, a silent corner
Not the worse for being
Twice searched.

Live to a great age
Each led—let each
Yield a little time

To the persuasive song
Of which each part
Must end;

Vicissitudes are so few
The old tree's talk
Brings small apes to the sapling.

Best teacher slight himself
Until his lightness becomes praise, the work
An exercise in time off

The stranger yourself comes unexpected
No stranger, the world's fool
Most happy.

Until the lightness be precise
Heraclitus over the kitchen fire—
"Come in, there are Gods here too

Don't be a stranger at the threshold"—
Parts of animals
The must of an ever

The infant laughing to its parent
Theory starts with that which is
Nature and art with what is to be—

Things that stay, and a taking off;
Breath by its passage breaks open
The nostrils' outlets.

Germ of each nature,
But its soul's end the animal's
Like the animal in a fable

Turned to stone, so scales
Feet, feathers
Used alike. Sponges

Virtually plants and
Not much more. Nature
Sorts from unbreathing things

To animals in unbroken sequence
Interposing life scarcely
Animal, jellyfish, sea-lungs

Their lives simply
Plants separated
From the ground

A tailsting
Nature gives it
To insects of fierce

Disposition—
To no others.
Hind legs of grasshoppers

Tho never the front seem to remember
The two long stem oars
By which a ship is steered.

To close their eyes
Some great birds
Crocodiles and frogs

Raise only their lower lid
A roll of skin
And as it contains

No flesh, like the prepuce
It does not unite
When cut.

The elephant clasps with
Nostril as a hand,
In water as with a diver's bell

A small bird has nothing fairly called
A nose, a beak for jaws,
Head and neck

Little, breastbone
Narrowed. An ox—horns of
Such length—he must

Walk backward to graze.
Brain is the cause of sleep
Why drowsy persons

Hang the head.
Flesh the organ of touch;
The animal becomes a plant

Its upper parts
Downward, its lower
Above.

All blooded animals
Have hearts
Origin and fountain;

Cut from Parnassus sedum
Which hung from rafters
Lives a considerable time.

Architecture—
Bricks, painting, timber etc—
But start and end: a house.

Man moved by his expectations
A beating heart
Not quite explained by the lung

His innocence his blood is water, his
Tears salt, his seed like the
Cells of seaweed, his

Bones the matter of coral
So that his God
Does not need advertisement

A half glimpse of
Your love—more pleasure than
In a bird's-eye view of the world

Love's leisure is
The prime end of all action
That Pharsalian mare called Honest;

Man should not work
At the same time
With his mind and his body.

Two rites burn for affection
It is your own
And you love it;

Touching community
Let this
Be the conclusion.

18

Further if politics be an art,
Most know nothing of peace
Supposing goods they contend for

Mean more than love
They regarded in making
Works

To occupy people
And keep them
Poor;

Nor does the toady
Thinking you're famous
Know we've endured.

As tho you sun your heart
Clod hear the gentle hop
The mix of sun and breeze

What knowledge forbids the tree—
That is not naked
Unashamed

Unclothed then
On the touchstone
Gold is proved

And in the fire
Soft is loyal
Until it see its proof.

There are emblems:
A long breath and a merry
What is said one sage

Old never sigh—Preserve you
—And you, to outlive long
The age I am

And die as I would do
—You wish me well.

In your need
Eyes search the voice
Voice urges eyes

Sure love is seen—
What time the Pleiades
Bay or elm poles

Freest of worms, the cranes'
Cry of the year, the soil
Light to be sowed.

Hope is a poor companion
Better a cap of felt
For dry ears in

Sleet winters blustering frost
Warmth for three. Need
Singer rival singer?

Intention betters contention.
Tibia the animal's legbone
Or old flute fleet of foot

Plays scales with no stutter
Might even refigure the Passion
'The blood of Christ, the blood of Christ

Why, my friends, the blood of
Christ is no more effectual
Than the blood of bulls and goats

Not a bit more not a bit.'
No waste beings crossed.
An economy of force

Unhurried grace. Not
Piercing nails, but as the
Flail's swipple or swingle

Coat perhaps lost sometimes harvesting
All in the life of old grandpa
Who still had some time to say *Ah*

Threshing grain by hand.
Your Bacchus bawled too much.
Heart disciplines the head

And with the blessings somewhere lower
Levels the eye, you're set
Not after the oxcidental child

Who when his parents
Spoke of the famine in China asked why
Couldn't they get bread in stores.

Briers beautify the john.
Colt in the field—Prancy Pants—
The advantage there the Great indoors

If you talk to yourself
Your love talks to you
Your music meets her words

Your child is always at the shoot of poplar;
'Is that enough water? there,
Suck that up'

As tho it is not known
As if it is not done.

ii

Why hop ye so, ye little, little hills?
And wherefore do ye hop?
It is because to us today, there

21

Comes the lord bis*hop*.
Why skip ye so, ye little, little hills?
And wherefore do ye skip?
It is because to us today, there
Comes the lord bis*hip*.
Why jump ye so, ye little, little hills?
And wherefore jump ye up?
It is because to us today, there
Comes the lord bis*hup*.
For 17 years and for 27
I have looked
Towards things thru (it better be *aside*—both)
The promenade
Not to evade
    —Can I help it if you're my father?
    —Look at the harbor.
One look at one august body, or
July ass.
Turning the head to look at
The people back of you
And the children in front, under, around
In summer the benches filled with people.
    —What interests you
    In the boats out there
    Or the lights the same lights
    And boats passing evening after evening?
    Now if their traffic stopped
    And the islands and shores moved
    We might be elsewhere.
    —And we are elsewhere.
The man on a bench facing the water
Writing a letter at sunset
Or a little after,
The last five evenings
Then reading his newspaper.
    —Surprising how long he can read the print after dark.
And what's in today's ashcan
The large leaves of newspaper.
Looking towards the span and towers of Brooklyn Bridge
Inclined towards Edward Hopper's angular search of shadows

We let two melodies run counter
The tacit always present and apposite
And all the other vociferous
Wryness of voice, sometimes
(How soon!) a young man's
Crescendo of a laugh
 —Wha-at!
 —Yes, he was thrown in a heap
Out of Carnegie Hall for yelling
Thru the great pianist's performance
Of the *Hungarian Rhapsody* "Is this necessary!"
And rose to the occasion
To the words
'I am a man needed but not wanted.'
As to how much one is needed it has been hard
To feel it these many years more than the light
                              of that joke.
 —A penny for?
 —Measure woo't burst the bean
Mere pulse is heir to
The bush of twigs in flower
The budding nuts elucidative stage
 —Wha-at
Must be the recording of the *Rhapsody*
I turned over and over when I was three
Until you were both out of patience he heard performed.
You remember the time when I told her
I could write Greek epsilon
So, CɛLIA—she refused to consider it
                    in the English lesson.
Years to sustain
A tone, not butter
 —I meant to mention there's a facsimile of
The First Quarto of *Pericles*
With a preface by Mr. P. Z. Round.
 —Not me; blind research
Only an excuse for laziness
Or the harmony of chances.
 —Another owned about 1750
By Charles Jennens the

Virtuoso, Handel's friend,
Another of the 1619 edition
Presented to the U. of Virginia
By Col. Thomas Mann Randolph
Son-in-law of Thomas Jefferson.
We sit down, two benches removed from the man with the paper,
If under the new promenade's flourescents
Just lit to hum a night
I pulse to notes a ten year dance
And let your dissonance counter them
How mean of me ridden by words
Always to think at first of being disturbed
                              by the dissonance
When the years make their order.
Order rains—Lucretius did not quite say that.
Torrential rain from interminable height
A planed splay
Thins, files
As does *lightning before one can say it, lighting*
A rain's slant on fog
Thru later thunderclaps
Horse torso off
Mural says to Tempera and
Mrs. Oil responds
   —Tuppence, Brumous
   For your thoughts
   —You said siphonate
   For hyphenate.
Alliterate often equals anyone can stutter.
And yet we are outwardly quiet.
   —Obviously characters
   He ambles
   She ambles with glasses
   That other with a feather.
   The old dowager again
   Crossing her ankles as she walks
   Reliving the ballet
   Ice cream (out of *Godey's*)
   Melting.
Good only when a grace is added

Radiations of quickest economies
Somehow last long.
    —That kid, banderlog singing.
'I think, madam, you can hardly
Be aware that your child's song
Is a cause of annoyance to the rest of us'
(The writer not what he says but whispers, like
Brother Harry) 'Let me impress upon you ..
One word you must inscribe upon your banner
.. *Loneliness.*'
    —Ha-ha the monkey of it.
No one should upbraid corpses
The French take their hats off to them.
We venerate our young
Instead of feeling as the Chinese of the last century
Proud of accumulating years ..
Our bones ripen it is true
For their ultimate repose .. but
How small a price to pay ..
For those adequate conceptions in whose possession
According to Spinoza's wisdom true felicity consists.
    —The afterglow in the two tallest Manhattan skyscrapers
    Has stopped glaring in my face
    They are cut of white cardboard
    On the blue
These blossoms nourished by something
As ugly as manure .. and the questionable gold
The world keeps putting .. into (my?) pockets—
His Quaker mother teaching them:
'Girls don't be too unselfish.'
As if their little lines and wrenched effects
Fluttered with the Savoyards out of the century's beginnings
For all of a world travelling in planes,
'Dear Mr. Gilbert, what is Mr. Bach composing now?'
'O dear madam, Mr. Bach is decomposing.'
The Gainsborough boy always ready to gain,
The Blue Boy uncommissioned,
Overheard "Sharp" Cathedral for Chartres.
    —Front is dress shirt
    Under is dirt.

Nostril singing
Milch and her co-warts.
Public walks projeks' rejeks
Deject subjeks no objek.
If with light head ..
From my poor love of anything .. But if
Listening behind me for my wit ..
The pricked horse's (inner?) ear.
The joys of my Old World have gone
From this new world—Ooçah—maybe the little Porto Rican boy
Still has them, waving the Flag with its
Fiftieth star for Hawaii.
Everyone now eats lamb with rose peas.
A dream of diet
Mostly the tie pin in the Iceberg (lettuce)
Recalls *The Stronger*, I didn't have the strength
To become your enemy
So I became your friend.
But I didn't have the strength to
Become your friend, so I became your enemy
Is just as true.
Roiled despite oysters
Shades of publicity
They dream their money to eat out fashionably
Orientals in tails crescents on their heads
Pastegem tiaras triumph with pomp thru the provinces.
The Chief of State for latrines or the Nations run by
                                a Doctrine
Feels a little younger at 85 —
And his best matched opponent
Who interpreted classically
Will never stand for the Herald in *Agamemnon*
Kissing his native soil as the enemy's arsenal—
Are alike being their own flues for natural gas,
Power never yet harnessed.
The second of uncertainty before the crescent's fluorescence
(Here history could not resist my sleep)
Fifty analysts puttered one hundred drinks round its
                                symposium couch
Beat stellar bottoms Emerson's *noble chemistry*

Poured out
Sunshine from cucumbers come true.
Or is the shine of any kid's pants seat
Reared from the floor
On a rainy day
A sign the solar universe
Is not running down,
Charlie befriending the kid
'There can't always be the orange outweighing the pea.'
An orange our sun—the pea, wee wee
'So I'm not afraid of all this atom business.'
For Saadi sat in the sun
Thanks .. his contrition ..
Saadi loved the brood of men .. said
It was rumored I was penitent
But what have I to do with repentance.
Not the unwashed lather startles,
The white of the unshaven beard
But that's as it is
When 'within a month' we overhear
'In-laws are outlaws.'
    —Shall we go home?
    —There's a sailboat, a sloop.
    —Still reading it
I wonder how far he's got
In that newspaper.
To his last best days on earth
The submarine that wouldn't stay down
The midge wing cycle of 1000 flaps per second
The Worm and Bug Committee's faith in the American farmer
Eastern Hemisphere versus American Beauties?
A distraction diffraction deal on the old firehouse.
    —Do we get up?
    —We *have* walked today
My lean old shanks hurt.
Twenty years since I've walked
From 12 Street home all the way
Across Brooklyn Bridge.
    —But it was worth seeing
The Old Fire House Museum on Duane Street.

A chaise whose two wheels carried the rolled rubber
Hose as if it were a lady
The Baltimore steam engine that sprayed
Water for 39 hours from its
Nickel and silver towers, only fifty years and
Museum pieces with the old gas mantle street lamp
Brought there maybe from C Street
Become fill-in for an avenue—
Unlit and under where they once lived—
We saw the rat lofts on Greene Street
The red iron-doored windows which never opened—
Fathers brothers and sisters
Walked towards them two miles six days a week
As operators pressers and finishers.
Overlook these parts of the score
The French conductor out of his ulcers
Advised his orchestra, for *look over*.
Aging as who does not alone
I remember another language
'I can't rear myself to *shwenk de wesh*'
(Rinse the wash)
Cloth of a greeting as friends met going to work
'A broch zu dir Semmele hust shayn a colt'
(The *a*'s Latin tho, the tone's sneeze Prospero's)
'Luck rack you Sammy you *have* a cold'
Cannot render it.
What father dreamed then of a grandson
Translating Latin sentences—
'The sword will be hidden in the man,
And the javelin in the bad boy.'
Or of Admiral Kickover
Red shoes and red do's,
Massive bleeding of a Prophet with *government property*
On his pyjama seat lacerating
Theological tarts and trembling hortatory
Out of pseudepigrapha, Fathers and canon
Contra bore with his dichotomy
Dick and a cot and o me
Isorhythm—I—so rhythm,
Dominations and angelic orders and kings

28

Coke and Coca Cola,
Against against a clay ton of editor
Who started as a shipping clerk
In a publisher's office and
Worked his way down to the top.
Corporations' incorporations
Ass up mentals: hay, bee, sea.
And proselytes ran off to give birth to Jesus.
Security? a leg's not safe
Even in bed it's seized with a crimp.
Satori oop my urethra noises
But not the muzjik's noises.
Or who dreamed then I would sit here
Envisioning a cellist
A tossed-off architectural façade
Every stroke of the bow
A frozen horizontal bar
His cello shined up like an old shoe
To look new, tied comfortably
For the used foot to move, or my word
A placed old shoe for a new foot.
Immortal, the hymn, the old man taller
Tapped his head a little preoccupied.
Belles-lettres—let her rather
See you come out simply
The less of all that the better
Memory can be a nothing towards something
A something towards nothing.
   —*You* have been dozing
   And *he* must have the eyes of a cat.
Nothing ran to a fire as fast as a thoroughbred
The Triangle fire how many corpses
Hasn't burnt them—fire traps, rat lofts
Iron-doored, boarded—at last—coming down.
In the infants and ladies whitegoods, shoddy remnant
                              textile district
The risen arcades of Richardson's spacious windows
Persist stacking reflected formations of clouds over
                              Lower Broadway
Melville (at the foot of Gansevoort) walked under them, Lanier

Lectured or played his flute at the Broadway Central, not too
                                        far a step
Into the past Irving's low town house with flower boxes, Twain
Smoking nearby about the time Henry James returned to take it
                                        in again
In a state of desire .. so as to .. care better .. just facts
Linen against an elegance when the Mews were still real stables
Behind the *American Classical* of Washington Square.
The extremes meet now in the televised education of the University
That has extended the Square to a Union where the flocks of
Grandsons and granddaughters who take courses eat—and learn
From the newspaper how Downtown Business is saving little
Old New York, where today of its past I reappeared
A permanent fixture some sibylline hindsight praising
                                        the grille work
Of Worth Street whitewashed to look as it was a hundred years ago.
And if the job is only half done, and business may never
                                        complete it—
O Pompeian florals—
An old sound track it was made W. C. Fields ventriloquially
                                        blare like the Sibyl: *Pay*
No attention to those dastardly fee-splitters.
Languidly precise Chopin playing to Mickey Mouse
In a world (of the survival of the misfittest?) where
You have to eat three times a day says our Cyrus—
                                two billion in holdings—
I can very well hear him doing it.
    —Nod off
    You had better sleep home
But today Sputnik over London says too-too-too
Over Paris ditto
Over Washington hah! hah! hah!
And Polaris says Whoobsk:
Dear whilom friend champing with the bad teeth of Rudaki
His laugh for the terns and the gulls fogdog
On The Hoe, Plymouth, England mimicked
The seadog with the two-year old—
'Tommy, what does Mr. Brown say?'
'Mr. Brown he says, *Boogar.*'
'And Tommy what does Mr. Ferris say?'

30

'Mr. Ferris he says, *Fook.*'
The violinist cannot wear a wrist watch when he plays.
love trouthe and . . wed thy folk
And may be breathing the style of no period
Chiefs of state now speak like simple men—
'A time for governments to step aside and
Let the people have their way' Dwight D for David.
(*People* but as the heart does not feel the common
                    noun rather each simple good)
'By pooling intelligence nets (laughing)
So we don't have to pay twice
For spying the same information
. . a hog under a sonar test
Wants to keep his fat sickness a secret,
Ashamed of it?
As to my saying we will bury you
Here is one city
Of Americans, literally to bury
Only this city *one* life would not be enough.
My face . . the wen is there
Nothing I can do about it,
I was born with it.'
After lunch: 'Even an animal
If you feed him becomes kind
Tho a Russian full of vodka
Could never reach the moon.
You are a nightingale . .
Singing it closes its eyes and hears nothing
And no one except itself,
Newsmen don't write anything
To provoke an incident . . spit in their
Eyes and they say God's dew.' Nikita,
                    second name?
G. says, Christian names? I haven't
                    met one in years.
Pullets, pewlitzers, dull bright fellows
Doctorates fifty years halted
While bathrooms don't have windows any more
Only $50,000 a year apartments
Permitting some outlook

31

To some aristocracy of defecation.
I lived it—and as in my sleep
He has read it *all*
With the giant scanner 30 years late—
(Never hurt to the friend's *good night*
Or thrived to the vines *good morning*)
But as in time it pays off
To see a tie between three ages
20, 40 and 60
While the oldest knows only
That he has breathed
20 years more than the older
And 40 more than the younger,
Is as in Cuba's cane or with snake dance
                          twining down on Kishi
Or as the Mau Mau who cannot blench
Before miscegenation
Or as the Queen of British barmaids
Before the Jury of her Pee-ers, Call
Me Hebe, that means goddess of youth, Dears!
Not with a telephone in his clothes closet
So to be private on a line to his broker, in case the
                                   margin
Drops the closeness of the walls and the door
Should sustain him.
    —Keep up your bright swords, for the dew will rust them
  God's my life—snoring—*no man can tell what.*
  —Look, if my gentle love be not rais'd up!
  The gent's gone I've inherited his *Times*
  Here read it yourself:
  —Protesting a tax on horsetails for bows
  M.P. was told 'I am glad he has
  an interest in violins. I thought
  he belonged to the wind
  rather than the strings.'
  —Take it along it's tomorrow's.
  Well I've never known anybody
  Can look or sound so weird without trying.
Tolerating accuracy for the greater inaccuracy
To perceive a law and to

Sheer from it without and with compunction
The thought only the mist of life.
   —Shall we walk the whole length while
       she is waiting?
   —Wait long enough and
   As the little old lady said
   Who transported her harpsichord
   On a sled lost in a storm
   One night to play for Tolstoy, years
   Before she used to be carried in blindfold
   To all her concerts—
   The horses find their way to the door.
   The hi-fi's are not out
   On the streets like the hurdy-gurdies
   Of 1910
   But by—
   —Landowska's nose, that's Bach's *Goldberg*
   Sounding off
   —They girdle the world.
No, let us not flatter ourselves ..
Not we .. invented loud noise—
There's her Music of the Past,
The Pole.
   —They all have their radios and phonographs on.
   If this street were made of records
   People would break pieces off the walls
   Of houses to play them.
Nero .. to Greece
For the music prize
With a claque of five thousand
Reinforced by half as many Roman athletes
To trigger the applause
Of an audience of one hundred thousand .. (Well)
Children are fond of stories
Which frighten them .. To
A monster concert .. at Dresden ..
1615 .. by command
Of the Elector of Saxony
One of my (Landowska's) compatriots
Raposki of Cracow ..

Brought from the Low Countries
(Breughel's spaces)
On a wagon drawn by eight mules
A counter-bass more than
Eight yards tall .. to reach its neck
Fitted .. a ladder .. (on a platform)
Many arms drew the huge bow.
This machine .. not enough for them
They conceived a counter-bass
An actual wind-mill
Strung with cables
Which four men vibrated
With a notched wooden beam.
Father Serapion worked
The great organ ..
A battery of mortars
Replaced the kettle drum.
Not the Golden Mean's
Calculus
As to when functioning noise
Deafens.
Stands for First Things
The Great Mother
Of our bodies .. her sons'
Minds in the Phrygian mode
Teaching the great earth
Hangs in space
Nor can earth
Rest on earth ..
Curetes .. a gang
With popcorn
Castanets, cymbals
Timpani, horn
Tibiae stimulate,
Trumpet—
    Let's go upstairs!
    What your Ludwig probably means
    By a point in space is a place
    For an argument
    Is that no one agrees

34

This is coal dust
And *that* a piece of coal,
I've the latter in my eye.
You cannot think illogically,
But the illogical is always logical:
Tape recorder—tape reason—is that *my* voice,
It is a philosophical-acoustical question
If anyone ever hears his own voice.
    —Now *I'm* sleepy.
The lobby blares a hi-fi
As to an imagined giant anatomical
    cast of inner ear
Tilted like Picasso's jeering horse's head in
His "Guernica."
In our corridor stand the lees of a milkfest
A dozen empty glass bottles
    —Our neighbors'
    Father and baby healthy
And before our own door
The paper, a letter, a postcard
The postcard from an old composer
Who teaches in his studio—
Which is his home—
And in his home,
Whose rare records not to mention limited
      editions of scores his young friends
Borrow (and sometimes sell but never buy)
And who with a twinkle in his eye
Says he prefers a long word to a short—
So *not* twelve-tone,
"Duodecuple."
Et bonum quo antiquius, eo melius
Really, the older a good thing, the better?
    —The letter:
    —*Thanks fer*
passover provender
       7
    gables
7 branches—
you never have

told me the history
of the li'll ole
    candy
      shoppe.
—Before Lunik Three
(the third)
Which is now nearer
The moon certainly
Than either to Moscow or New York
Choctaw *oke* or *hoke* equals *yes.*
And the history of the shoppe—
Say it was
With care, with care
My friend in a world where
Not all saints are friends
    —What's tha-at!
    —A diva singing six feet of uplift
    The *helden* soprano whose horse
    Fell to the stage floor
    When she leaned her elbow on it and
    Stood on oblivious singing Brunhilde
    (A true story.)
Man in the moon stand and stride
On his forked goad the burden he bears
It is a wonder that he does not slide,
For doubt lest he fall he shudders and sheers.
When the frost freezes much chill he bides
The thorns are keen to tear his tatters to shreds.
Is no one in the world knows when he sees,
No but it be the hedge, what weeds he wears.
Whither trusts this man what the way takes?
He has set one foot and his other before
For no behest he hastes can he see me nor move
He is the slowest man that was ever borne.
Where he was of the field and pitched stakes
In hope his thorns would stop up his doors
His twibill had other cuttings to make
Or all his day's work would be there forlorn.
This same man up high ere he was there
Where he was born and fed in the moon

Leans on his fork as a grey friar
This crooked canard sore in his dread
It is many a day gone that he was here.
I know of his errand, he has not sped
He has hewn somewhere a burden of brier
Therefore some hayward has taken his pledge.
If the pledge is forfeit bring home the brush
Set forth thy other foot, stride over sty
We shall beg the hayward home to our house
And put him at ease for our mastery
Drink to him dearly of foul good booze
And our Dame Dowse shall sit by him
And when he is drunk as a drenched mouse
Then we'll redeem the pledge from the bailiff.
This man does not hear me tho I cry to him
I know the churl is deaf the Devil take him.
Tho I yell up high he will not hie
The lost lazy lout knows nothing of law.
Hop out Hubert in your hose magpie!
I know you are marshalled up to your craw
Tho I rage at him till my teeth are on edge
The churl will not down ere the day dawn.

iii

The human son fathered by man and the sun sleeps
As with the sun sleeps nights, but the earth
Not quite the defense of "Still it does move"
Goes on in my heart. His mother—
They go on in your heart. You sit
By and here's the Korean King who
In the first half century—the style is—'of our Era'
Sailed his half-cylinder of bark from the mainland
('In Korean,' said the Methodist native, *paulownia* wood')
Skirted the rapids, landfall, and there turned it down
To dry and again over to string and play it
His harp in the isolation of his island;
As the child's half-size violin
Sounded thru the test in a wind tunnel.
Or as you may judge my Shakespeare theme— *'Love sees?'*—

37

When love and eyes go together
Blessed, blessed reasonable idiot—
The old spinet we have yet to buy
Mozart's dissonance, the dead season
That returns with four seasons.
It is with the world in our hearts
As it was with him as a child
When asked to roll up his shirt sleeves
To keep cool in the torrid heat
He refused yet under protest said
"All right, but remember it's cold."
Only in Shakespeare is there
Such reconcilement of the abstract and the actual.
It is in the earth of our hearts sometimes as in the world
As with old faces of soldiers in their teens whimpering
That tonight gone may bring peace to the ridge of
                                    outpost Harry
Tomorrow, the shell-fire's twenty rounds a minute stop
For the dead buddy, its boot stuck out;
As with one wounded brought a cross
And asked did he recognize it, answered
"An instrument of torture."
And it is on earth as with you by me
Sometimes a foolish world but pleasant:
(— You needn't run up and down stairs
For what you forget so often,
I'll bring it to you
—That's all right for my new logic.
—'Batter up, Grumpa Marrump'
—Your idea of novelizing
The pernicious being
Of the little girl
Sounds interesting if
Not fascinating
You know how I feel
About some little ones.—
That was years before
The lyric poet made an art of violating.
Now as most anyone
Writes to play the bass drum

On everybody, and oneself
Seems the exception moved
By the intimacy of one response
There will have to be a
Redefinition of writing.
'An older sister an English beauty
Called Violet second name Wentworth,
Drawled *Want-wart*, with a young
Man piercing her brightly, I sell
Saddle leather—O then, stretched to *than*,
You *must* be rich!'
—He used to talk about
His art and his God and his fiddle.
Then one day when he
Was supposed to play in Philly
We told the musicians he
Didn't hold a union card and
They walked out
So now him and his God
And his fiddle
Are in the local.—
Two hundred years ago
His alma mater
Under charter of the King
Set among the gravestones of Trinity,
A hundred years later
Moved to the site of the old
Deaf and Dumb Institution,
After expanded to the Heights
The library on ground
Formerly occupied by
Bloomingdale Insane Asylum.)
It is with earth as I say—
Seeing because tears are
Forbidden to these eyes,
Forget it tho I tell it to you
Say nothing to no one not even to me again
Unless some luck attends it
Then it will happen to you
Unlike the quartet

Of daily garbage collectors
Storming after
'Barrel E, Barrel A, Barrel D, Barrel G'
That you will be happy for the young
Who worded that foursome
String loose, and for his innocence
Careless not to understand we have aged.
Not to share with our age the same weakness
.. the commodity wages not with the danger
.. to live quietly and so give over.
.. sung, and made the night bed mute .. and
                    the lonely listener,
prose clothes the poem
.. world-without-end bargain in.
And take upon's ..
Who loses and who wins; who's in, who's out ..
As if we were God's spies ..
If we didn't both like to talk
   there would be scarce use in talking at all.
Less noise the fewness of three together
We age who will not suffer
The shame put upon youth
Naked an all-around bug on face of white rock
                              in the sea,
Asking with letters written on it, "Do you love?"
Come to that sea and air
The stars of their worlds
Looking at him with unconcerned eyes.
What brought it up—
Forget—
M. said, whom I read
About at P's age, sixteen
To give an exhaustive
Account would need
A less brilliant pen than mine
No one in history or legend
Died of laughter, add the smile of
A dying they call civilization.
I cannot forget it,
To have said unprovoked

To sixteen years rushing on seventeen
You can't win affection
By wishing your opponent to drop dead—
While the wish may be there
There is no defense—
Pill-and-Envy
Mud's Son
All he has to do is to sit down
And he looks like Michelangelo's *Moses*
Preempted of the beard
By all future egalitarians—
Pretends like his valet
The great know how to wait—
Airing his finds
Of painters who seek the greatest canvas coverage
For their slightest posterior temperatures
Their condescension too great a responsibility
For their itch to probe their heat itself
Not all cheeks pinched in public look red—
But they too perhaps may be said to feel the earth.
Had he said it to me—what answer?
An astronomer gazes at stars
Is it *against nature* as Inthehighest said
To sleep by day and be awake at night
If one's trousers are subsidized out of the world.
Downcast because alive?
It could be simpler, granted.
As when the Catholic child
Saw the Infant in the crèche
After the annual wait
The second Noël he remembered
—He doesn't seem to have grown any,
Who was his father, a carpenter,
Why doesn't he build him a bed?
Or as the architect
—You can get culture
If you will skip education—
Interlocked his fingers
To illustrate reinforced concrete
And then made a pier and lintel

Of his old hands
To show where corners chip off.
Admitted, my modest philosophers—
No, common sense is not
What we find in the world,
Instead what we put into it,
Ourself lost in the things we make
Does His nth sense take care of them.
One swallow does not summer our nights
Calling up the hush of the new born baby brought
        home after its mother's confinement
A shoot of plant grows a root on the ledge of
                        the kitchen sink
Times the rests you play solitaire
The visible paradise of the dying physical soul,
Vico's *intellegere* from *legere* to collect greens
The shock of first leaves their sibilance
The oldest story aching on love
Disserere to discuss to scatter seed,
You who will keep possessions to a minimum
—Bach, Mozart, Shakespeare—and most others
        had no need to bother—
Only the notes that see,
But for your pages you tore up
Of which I pasted the pieces
How else may we prove together
That the blindness of love was the eyes' refusal
To see what they let get by.
Opal to the fire of the sun
The small shell-like ears
That my heart knows will never be the world's wide
                        commonplace,
Constant in saving intention from wrath
Not a televised or radar heaven,
Their haven the opera—your song after 17 years
                you know was
For voices and lute.
Dian's argentine, simple unclouded thing
M .. m, night's mute, the slightest sound made with closed lips
The whole tale—

You are not to throw out your music
Grafted to the adequate,
Seen as the heart's beat for more hearing
Nothing stronger to displace it
The certainty which a third when revery
        turns to talk must see.
Oh well say it lightly
—As he approaches six feet
His pants lose inches to increase the range
Of his mouth when talk opens it.
And you—you say to me—lover more like H. J.
As days track in days and their says
Grow more devious, all his girth
That accrued to him outwardly disappears inside you
As the great numbers to resignation
In every strike unfed, unclothed and unread,
Make no boast
As to *Being everywhere*—the table? the chair?
No not a thing. It pervades? O, then,
                        a skunk,
They can't understand intellectual larking.—
If I collect these things to live
It is that I think my eyes, ears and head are still good.
If I quote it is myself I have seen
Coming back to learn conveniently from one book:
It is not night when I do see your face.
Why so:
'I make my money by my hobby.'
His very honey is his lobby.
What do the well-off envious of us
Expect us to have done all these years, to stand still?
There was affection so affluent
It used our lives for one long book thru all
                        our books,
Now their rivalry lives forever, why should
                        each grudge?
I paid taxes. "List all dependent on you for support:"
Me. "Relationship:" poet.
The blood's music repeats: "cellar door" (1926),
(1956) "*Neither/nor*, nor *and/or*"

Attesting an exchange between an intellective portion
Of head and that part it calls music
Meaning something some time to come back to a
                                        second time,
As if there were shoes to cobble
I cobbled, my father was a cobbler,
Honor a word gone out of English
        wove out of Bottom the weaver,
Richard Flecknoe on *Pericles*:
"*Ars longa, vita brevis*, as they say
But who inverts that saying made this play."
Was he saying it was a bore, or rather the opposite
That the life is longer than the brevity of its art.
The lines of the song *Pericles* that ends so many times: *life*.
Our thoughts .. ours .. their ends not our own,
As the eye looks to outlive its error.
And it is in the earth as in the auditorium of
                        Memphis—not Egypt—Tennessee:
An arena divided equally by a curtain
Into two amphitheatres,
In the one they stage wrestling matches, in
                the other hold concerts—
Often together the same evening;
In the one spectators in the smoke of the third balcony
Are so dense they appear painted
Like Michelangelo's hordes of the Judgment
                                in the Sistine Chapel;
In the other perhaps the *saraband* of
Bach's Second Partita for Violin Alone plays
As the wrestlers thud.
Pantsfullofit. Taine said as a point of good style,
'Only one thing revolves around—
A *** around a ***'—
3 stars around 3 stars—
But his touch fails as it's coarse,
The King is a thing, says Hamlet
Shocking only the fox.
My sweet unworded, we fall into disuse,
The sense that attached to us persists
Despite the yellow page of local history

44

Has quickly turned over, breath
Evaporates so slowly
    in tiniest droplets of mist
Night less it tells again
Your mother's story of the blacksmith shoeing
The horse, and the little frog lost in the stable
Toddles up one leg held up too for shoeing.
You who detest perfume read me of
Attar of roses banked as collateral in place of gold
1,100 lbs of essence valued at $800 a pound—
The Bulgarian rose the conquering Turk rode
Out of Persia—in the damp season rain intensifies
Their fragrance, the hot sun makes them grow faster
Than they can be picked, a harvest of roses before dawn
The second hour most of May thru early June
Twenty-five days
When the drivers of loaded carts ride embedded in blossoms,
Profusion—
4000 lbs of roses yield one lb of essence.
The weight of the air is heavier than we are, and
By chance looking into the stereoscope I have picked up
Brings back our other summer:
TOURISTS, *Hotel Moonglow*, Niagara—
Nature has been kind, so
This is what they did to nature.
There come back not in the order of an itinerary
Jefferson's slave quarters in his natural air-conditioned
                      cellar at Monticello;
Washington's directly in his view from Mt. Vernon's portico
Prove him the less gadgeteer, the simpler founding father;
Magnolia and rhododendron: trees! The South's crepe myrtle,
The Collection's Amati they let him try out in the Library of
                       Congress
Mimosa, blossomed mountain laurel, Arcangelo—
The mad kept way out there in a circle as he played—
Corelli, Jannequin's song
In the shadow of curtain behind curtain of trees
And then chased the birds. Travelled with
Western camellia, deodar
Tall trees and waterfalls

45

But falls and falls of tall trees
Douglas firs, redwood
A horseshoe promontory
White face of an animal or a peak
Twin of the white of Gilbert Stuart's
Portrait of Washington.
Oregon: Crater Lake saw
No order except its intense blue that
Clouds over it do not change—
Other blue lakes clouds cover black.
Thoughtful eyes of landscape disinclined to die,
Sages of sheaves of analects
Who had lasted to taste trees grow,
Far from the misnamed temples
Of Grand Canyon's absurd sunsets
Evoking slaughter of Indians
In a burlesque of Indians.
The tourist emerald of Lake Louise
Set in the glacier,
Brown bear cubs on the porch of the one hotel
Paul called them kadota figs.
Canadian azaleas at the rail fences of the small town
Yellow Iceland poppies a sage might love,
An unnamed pink weed, some purpling by gray
And what they called for all of
A crest and crush of colors
            poor man's flowers.
Fortunate to board a train with a drawing room: "A"—
Could our fathers see it what would they say
To its bright comforts of steel and chrome
Polished to look mild
As we looked out, on to Winnipeg,
At the soft mountains of Canmore
Thrown-up rocks, but traced with archaic noses
With ancient sisterly eyes in their faces
Green held, holds slanting up to them
So green a shade of gray
As tho a tree were painted path.
Smoke from a heap of leaves burning
Around a tree trunk

Rises thru morning sun in
Overhanging branches
So that its spring rays
Return on themselves
As spokes of smoke.
And with our early thought for dawn
This late hour the literal stereoscope
Has no use before our eyes' looks that blend
                              of themselves,
The human son and the sun sleep as tho
                              interchangeably—
And you may remember how only a few years ago
You intended a small boy to light a masquerade
As a Chinese sage with blue whisk for beard
Shoe string for mustache and your black dress
For ceremonial robe. It is then
Not a world of four words—last things—
Not of a far-fetched fear that when the Chinese
Adopt the Latin alphabet
All language might be one.
For it is what each says exactly to each
That matters to us most—
Then the K'in plays its principles from nature,
Fields' earth, skies' round
Flat and dome
Length a ratio to a leap year
Thirteen studs, moons
Five strings of twisted silk ply of elements
Five notes planets from the lute pear—
Mercury, Jupiter, Saturn, Venus, Mars—
Yü—North's black winter water
Chiao—East's blue spring wood
Kung—Compass' center yellow prevails
        over all four seasons' earth
Shang—West's white autumn metal
Chi—South's red summer fire.
So what if we don't know Chinese
Don't we become legend
Come back to read from one book
I do see your face—

The note *Kung* rules,
Shang ministers,
Chiao peoples,
Chi attends its state
Yü, to solid objects,
Dealing from a household
Each art deals from the structure
        of its own house—
Earth's yield and work
Use to the used
Evil's quelled, heart beats right
Desire mates tone:
Our bodies know more than our heads,
The windows open on music
The venetians stop rattling.
We talk after the fishermen in *Pericles*
Who banter their verse
Droll roll and gambol of a playful
      fish of the playful sea—
Shakespeare skeptical of most music
Considering the longest preparation of it turns out
                             fleeting.

This work shall live this night.
"He that doth ill hateth the night."
Only *he*; this night is courtly
Our own performance of Gagaku
A refinement so ancient it was never primitive
The dance makes space
(Not their ballet frittered thru it, frittering
                  it away)
The light shares it, sun
Tilled earth air
We they the old man and old woman dance
The Monkey Dance with white masks
(*Able* the sensible rhesus thrown into
                that space
His reins neither Abel nor Cain)
They are a bit ridiculous?
Slits—eyes?
A disturbed music all the way to the sun.

48

Where? Everywhere. The air is around them.
There off—the mountain is peace.
The music is one note
The Monkey God comes down from
    the mountain to watch. He stands still.
His face is his mask.
The Monkey is God
And seems to say
Don't scan
It is simple
To measure the dance
The foot up
Must come down
Unsaid appears said
And four feet standing together
In wish be raised
A lover's body turned as a phrase
And its multiples.
But clumsy
If you count and stress 10 in a row
You have also the time of 10 not stressed
Not seen
How does that work out as a system of 10.
Figure it out
But don't dance to stamp now
For those who will dance after you
Again.
The Monkey God stands still and appears to smile:
Stop rushing me to your graves
So that there appear instants
Between no word and no word
When there are gaps between things.
Should you never speak or step
You mean the same things to me.
Foolish to dare dance for all of a world
As for your killing chores to say
For the beloved body that has not stayed
                              its mind,
When I die you can take over and rush ruins
    the whole hog.

Do I hear your steps say together
If human life were a mountain or a flower
It could love itself—
Tho you are seeded
So the sun warms your bodies as one.
Your human son sleeps and does not care
That your steps say your three bodies are one.
Oldish man, frail, a
Yellow slip of paper
On which a song buds,
Wife who cannot always
Rush a song her way to say
It was after all
   not a bad life
Your eyes look at hands
     lips seem to
     touch.

iv

Too heavy
for
my
breast pocket—

small as it
is
in
my wallet

the size of
a
vis-
iting card

but holding
no
such
thing, no need

to tell her
who
has
found the scrip

my resourc
es
for
my son who

has looked in-
to
it
—wha-at—you

will find—by
your
own
eyes, by strength

plainly spoke-
n
yet
pardon me

whose chase is
this
world
and we in

herds the game,
when
I
spur my horse

content and
an-
ger
in me have

but one face
to
the
music his

own hoofs made
lived
in
her eye love

and beyond
love
or
reason, wit

or safety—
five
owned
snapshots my

father, moth-
er,
two
the fiddler's

at nine and
a
half
my young wife

in peacock
feath-
ered
hat the year

he was born
(vi-
o-
lin label)

"Jakobus
Stain-
er
in Absam

prope Oe-
ni-
pon-
tam 16-

56"
if
I
lose my ad-

dress, a phone
my
broth-
er's latest,

all written
mi-
nus-
cule on odd

scrap paper
no
room
it goes down

carefully
hy-
phen-
ated each

syllable
pours
in
the measure

53

maze I planned
song
long
since and that

would not be
hur-
ried
life into

dust (who can-
not
feel
nor see the

rain being
in't
knows
neither wet

nor dry)—a
blank
check
not for much—

two dollars
held
to
the spine of

my wallet
by
a
rubber band—

next to some
breath
cop-
ied clear and

such green lines
rush
on
root *Go, fresh*

horses the
bar-
ber's
last haircut

Thoth the price
went
up,
seraphs light

cherubs high
seas
smoke
streak Chinese

whips stage sym-
bols
for
horses, on

this bed face
a
sleep
Hop o' my

Thumb lady-
bug
wake
the things left

mastery—
by
my
short life my

body to
this
thanks
tender her—

it *lets*
offerers—
tandaradei

'THE
TOO PAUL
HIS CAT

V

Naked sitting and lying awake
Quiet held near to speak,
Walking past each other not to step
Over their own bodies
Slender summit most night
Envelope of floral leaves'
Twilight when all seams sun
The same either night or day
Travels the raised blind
Lights the view.
From five contiguous windows of a tenth floor, as on
Sundeck in the cabin of a boat,
Full cycle
Remembered innocent desire *from eleven to ninety*
Lets innocence to age.
Remembers family of its young days
Incidents as tho they were now
Hands clasped over four knees
Sealed by the eyes,

The embrace
When *children in some kind*
Desire looked until it saw
On the next roof
A story lower,
Its decorations a corbie gable
Topped by a squatted unicorn
That's flanked by four flues
Machine made shapes—
Chess set castles
Of the same soft stone
As the stone-scarfed
Ridiculous near-horse
A sagging bag of meats—
No art may divine
Why it's there
Unless it be honored
As some curious attempt
Of desire before it looks
Pulses and grows near.
Surcingle—Sir Single.
And comes to:
Behind the five windows
The light let to no hour
Becomes all neighborhood,
A valentine: that jewel box: that heart.
Then are seen
The terraces of other houses,
Courts ten floors beneath,
Penthouses, tended gardens
On other roofs of
Gingerbread shapes
All periods,
Antennas, a city of
Quoins, stringcourses,
Rustications,
Ogee arch, spandrel,
Drum, dome, lantern,
Veronese parapets,
Florentine towers,

Siena marble, gold,
Moorish fretwork
(*For what we lack we laugh*)
Crowns of
Two towers
Each an hexagonal arcade
(Lit at night)
Married to the ends of a prolonged façade.
Not to be outdone
To the right of it
The steep wall of the world's largest hotel
Discounts the two towers
To tourelles as it were
In the lowest drop of a falls
Inverts them to the lowest of diving bells
Tuning a lost voluntary
.. your sweet music .. last night ..
Always between the pattern of roofs
    there is water hidden and open below
That brings the bridges to span it
        piers and boats,
Whole
Quiet
Visible and invisible
Waterfront
Of the fantastic island
To the North
That but for a little green
Is entirely buildings
And pavement
Holding such sights
As a café front
Composed of a mortared
Giant champagne glass
Overflowing a coruscation
Of rocks;
All such instants
Watched over
By the Empire State
As tho it were

A bestiary
Whose crowned fable
Of animal
That goes up
Is its bullet head
Naked and unashamed
Pulsing rays of
A searchlight
One forgets
How many miles
Radius into other states
That light the nights
Of the young in the woods,
Pompons, ferns, petiole,
Hair-like needles,
Grass that must outlast
The Egyptian queen
—age cannot wither
So brief is not brief
Not brief is so brief
Quiet once taught to speak

The embrace
Of the beloved
That know
Nothing else
Within or
Without,
Incapable of
Conspiring
Together

Not of words,
Eight definitions
Seven axioms

Does not think:
Cause
Limit
Substance

Attribute
Mode
Absolute
Need
Eternity
Essence
Conception
Sequence
Knowledge
Identity
Idea
Negation

(Launce)
To
Stand-under ..
Under-stand ..
all one

Or two, three
Numerous
Only the image of a voice:
Love you

14

beginning *An*

An
orange
our
sun
fire
pulp

whets
us
(everyday)
for
us
eat
it
its
fire's
unconsumed

we'll
not
fire
there
rocketed
that
poor
fools
be
sure

moon
loon

bless
light
he
pees
pea
blossom
sun's
peer.

*First of
eleven songs
beginning An*

in the
middle of
solar winds

paddle satellite
let some
be unnumbered

the night
of the
hours the

24 all
of a
day the

words you
count what
words you

leave out
that count
go backwards

Ranger VII
photos landing
on the

moon
how deep
its dust?

crater whose
base is
shoal? Egypt

Sumer's works
whose foot
has disappeared?

The works.
Hallel ascents
degrees vintage

songs planned?
40 years
gone—may

ear race
and eye
them—I

hate who
sing them?
while I

have being?
and when
you look

least our
thoughts run
together Aristippus

spittle seed
bore—he
and now

she—my
bane foe
hymn yet

new call
how great
you are

made and
all you
have lavished.

Dark heart
it wear
long under

where 'familiar
vague sounds
exchanged every

waking—not
arguing with
a lunatic

either—alone
in the
wilderness concentrated

fought with himself
his intelligence
perfectly clear'

a gentle
christening "civil
rights" disobedience

humbled in
murder 'I
saw it I

heard it
I saw
her his

death and
her sorrow
do you

understand I
saw them
heard them

together she
was never
so sad

as when
she laughed
but always

laughed when
she was
sad' As

one frost
to another
keep warm.

Throw bottles
jeering at
their funerals

sweep down
by pressure
hoses, the

cutting streams
strip the
bark off

trees four
little girls
bombed 'better

trust an
unbridled horse
than undigested

harangue'—*Crazy*
white man!
high altitude

tests as
the South
shanty sure

one empty—
full scene.

'Fly which
way shall
I fly

whose eye
views all
things at

one view
in the
precincts of

light grateful
smell old
Ocean smiles

without thorn—
or happiness
in this

or the
other life
not in

the neighboring
moon Paradise
of Fools—

moon risen
on mid-noon
on his

side leaning
half-raised
leaves and

fuming rills—
space may
produce new

worlds, landscape
snow or
shower—Thee

Tsīyōn feet
nightly visit
sharpening in

moonëd horns.
I started
back it

started back
what thou
seest what

there thou
seest thyself
with thee

it came
and goes
but follow

me. Whom
fliest thou?
whom thou

fliest of
him thou
art. Millions

of spiritual
creatures walk
the earth

embryos and
idiots
from

root
springs lightly
the green

stalk freely
love full
measure only

bounds excess
and if
one day

why not
eternal days
Distinct with

eye heaven
ruining from
heaven and

68

the great
light of
day yet

wants to
run night
silence sleep

listening till
song end.
Created each

soul living
each that
crept forthwith

the sounds
and seas
and callow

young intelligent
of seasons
the smaller

birds with
song solaced
the woods

nor then
the nightingale
ceased among

the trees—
in pairs
they rose

they walked
those rare
with heart

and voice
and eyes—
subdue it

a World
zone thou
seést powdered

with stars
and freed
from intricacies

the prime
wisdom what
is more

is fume.
Happier than
I know.

Flung rose
flung odours
sung spousal

easier than
air with
air in

at his
mouth all
things that

breathe (stupidly
good the
hot hell

that always
in him
burns) hath

tasted envies
not, song
each morning

of thy
full branches
into Heaven—

lost Paradise
Death on
his pale

horse unhide-
bound cold
ground long

day's dying
his own
hand manuring—

Paradise how
shall we
breathe in

air
bent on
speed black

gurge human
from human
free so

many laws
argue so
many sins

till over
wrath grace
shall abound

hope no
higher tho
all the

stars thou
knew'st by
name.'

As at
the scroll's
first hanging

found my
own initials
looking in

Ryokan drop
down almost
as one

might breathe
in the
falling snow

of its
blossoms the
sound forgot

'I only
see what
sounds—R

shied as
an admirer
asked a

memento of
his hand—
maybe you

realize the
Ryokan scroll
is public

upside down'

Freak hard
to see
here I'll

check when
I go
home.

Emptied out
of the
petals whichever

way they
fall, as
the earth

heaped in
all senses
but not

the worst
erratum
for 'the

blossoms **to**
fall up'
for the

under round
of our
world had

TOP marked
hopefully for
a printer.

Good gout.
'Not sedulous
to indite

not tilting
furniture not
able to

quaff huge
tankards lustily
did not

insult only
preferred Truth
to King

—mere
move from
one residence

to another
a cause
of sickness—

(*had* travelled)
after I
had put

on board
a ship
the books'

—Italian, yes?
—No (*dozing*)
—Italian, yes?

—No. Jewish
from New York City.
'Retreated to

74

a pretty
box, the
beyond: myrtles—

love was
not in
their eyes—

past who
can recall
nothing is

here—for
tears a
sense variously

drawn from
one verse
into another

not in
the jingling.
To open

eyes *make*
them taste.'
Would make

soldier of
his A-
string?

'nobody not
a hut
standing, if

a gang
of *thick-lips*
armed suddenly

took to
travelling on
the road

catching the
white swine
right and left

I fancy
every farm
and cottage

hereabouts would
get empty
infra dig

only there
houses had
fallen in

and I
don't like
work I

like what
is *in*
the work'

Innocence *in-*
nocere not
to do

hurt to
and the
news the

same shame—
night of
the winter's

relieved only
by the
newspaper strike

not a
paper for
the last

17 weeks
to bring
its inanities

and horrors
home as
if a

miracle might
devastate the
economy, advertising,

theatre, the
arts' powerful
business, installment

buying and
selling, the
sparkling water

the cold
war—*abi*
gesunt abi

"alright" my
father'd say
and as

the Irish
Boston factory
worker forr

77

Ted's campaign
'Teddy I
hearr you

haven't done
a day's
worrk in

yourr life—
you haven't
missed a

thing—'
and if
the candidate's

family were
all loyal
to 'each'

other as
they seemed
to the

voters, better
than no
family. Why

not 'speech
framed to
be heard

for its
own sake
even over

its interest
of' (de-)
'meaning'

Wedged blue water
sky and ice
of zero weather

incunabula gilt head
cane, feeling of
longer spring light

king rag paper
pedlar, horse-finch, harbor
piers and points

of land jutting
from islands, land
containing the water

YAMASHITA LINE
on the dock
a long dolly

two stacks of
dinghies—
paper matchstick 'like'

lavender-white-navy
blue funnel in
port—crates to

be shipped bound
by the Port
Authority railroad

which ho's to
the waterline—a
fresh wharf coming

up, first stakes—
and the monstrous
engineering works or

79

a float (?) chiefly
cranes, 3 pylons
before a cabin

in steel tower—
floes (pact) ice
Brooklyn (Japan)

or a Hokusai.
Eagle knocker above
footlocker Chinese wind

chimes no plant
grows but the
void for it—

Alone: the few
minutes I breathe
terrace to watch

the harbor burn—
and I think
B's Chomei—stone—

the friends are
more important to
me than my

song the friends
don't see it
surely don't act

here, curry-spun-dense about
a clubfoot—young,
Swift had no

scholaress—old, afraid
to ease liquid—

I'm son of
a guileless presser:
Suffenuses, soon *footprints*

on the sands
of time, sands
of time one

the less, better
sands *of* time

not
a
long
fellow.

Where are my
distance glasses, reading
lenses, focus of

the aging—I
stumbled into the
TV—'you want?

to be on
television'—C.

WINTER CANINE HOTEL.
Why should a
dog winter, not

enough summers? bobbing
of trees mushrooming
up clouds. Loves

what he plays
L'Enlèvement d'Europe—
the Defoe of

Europe's jakes where
voids all her
offal outcast progeny,

kokoro—mind you
recordari re + *cor*
my dictionaries—heart

recorder plays house
to make peace
with a fiddle.

The child once
cried twice first
on hearing how

he was born
and again one
wail when his

grandpa died, remaining
afterward unmoved by
obituaries, found the

only way to
outlast their authority
is to outlive

them and shortly
had some sensible
criticism of post

doctorals whose wives
covet influence or
wall-to-wall carpet—

rather to wood
like "the theatre's
an intellectual hogpen"

(some pianist peas
so tinkle) and

America's diagnosed Indian
summer Melville's windy
quite understandable there's

a lot of
wind around, James'
persisting for all

he prefaced revisions,
Twain's Jim with
integration *behind* him,

Adams' *History* his
progenitors' lives—Hawthorne's
a chair (grandfather's)

the scarlet rest
dull or horrible,
Irving storaged the

storied sketch, Whittier—
wittier authority doily
its *lo* well—

low who hid
him untried touch
ax hold body

Song of Myself
11 my Shih-king,
I *was* Kagekiyo.

'That thunders in
the Index' Imagine,
said Celia, selling

the movie rights
to *Bottom: on
Shakespeare*. No

index was whole
so our index
will sometimes lead

us to us
Job's Lo and
his strength—'stones'?

no song summers
but loyal hush
lull—motor *off*.

My loves alone
tap untabbed possibilities
Of "formal education"

the Low Library's
Doric columns a
boy's first sight

on a starry
night—their elephantine
bases toe nearly

all that remains—
stairs, a friend's
ascent, transparency eating

paper—the dead
friend always the
other side of—

River when I
look—except my
life except my

loves I have
read and forgotten
en canimus listen

we are singing
*claruit semper urbs
nostra musica,* our

city sets forth
in music—in
the dark backward

glib as who
when thing or
life was good

chattered 'it sings'
drew up facile—
doubt true skeptic

your *everyday* is
doubt, better not
know the family

tree, be spared
a feeble smile
eulogy lights on

Bach's necrolog from
half-wit aunt
aging child 'knew

not right hand
from left, brothers
the Lord glorified.'

Dim eye looks
where the lively
mind once skipped,

85

at five I
heard in Yiddish
Prometheús Desmótes chanted,

Seb Bach at 14
mastered Phocylides' "spurious"
Poíema Nouthetikón in

Greek, '*Mind you
Poem*' "half-Jewish from
the Pentateuch"—thumbed

also the genuine
kaì tóde Phokulídeo
this too kindling

key to Phocylides?
Clifftown stands civil
above mad Nineveh—

bread first then
virtue—justice whole
virtue—Lerians evil

all, not Procles
he's Lerian—rich
and no delight

in word or
action—middleman lives—
lady was dog,

bee, pig, horse—
or had Seb Bach
no need to

sneer Maria Barbara
in the choir.
And see in

Bach's life what
I lived thru
which I could

not possibly see
40 years sooner
reading it then

not *looking* for
it—*Cythringen* (little
zither, lute) son,

a Lammerhirt (his
shepherding mother) had
some means, station,

her father in
the municipal council,
for music thrives

only where there
is *some* means
(when a kid

your old man
declaimed reams of—
for pennies of

East Side Italians)
and the rest
of Bach's "life"

so familial and
familiar how he
envied Christoph's clavier

pieces by moonlight
read his Hebrew
Greek or Latin,

clavier lessons (something
C's piano) no
organ his own

his discant voice
breaking fled into
those high notes

into cantatas
Passions and
tho he played

fiddle near cradle
preferred the viola
in concert attent

the middle of
harmony in his
position to hear

and enjoy—in
his ma's family
(also) some distant

relative not even
professional had made
and played a

fiddle. Who urged
no less than
music, we innocents

are somewhat heroes—
no uncle quarreling
to run your

musical Center as
Seb's did—Bach's
advantage later. *Capriccio*

sopra la lontananҙa
del suo fratello
dilettissimo, departing

brother, and youthfully
righteous affronted the

ҙippelfagottist for bassooning
in wrong time,
we'll suppose that

when even earning
money tired, slipped
out of the

organ gallery into
a beer cellar.
Waiting his lifetime

for patience to
join a Societät
der Musicalischen Wissenschaften

(o Science) his
student who had
dedicated "the" doctoral

thesis to Bach
had founded not
for "practising" performers

but theoretical members
to circulate dissertations
postfree among fellows.

French music then
as *current,* "ornament"
hid calculus of

Leibniz, affliction of
Voltaire's Jacques, his
news Bach's news

Thirty Years' War
some thirty years
before Seb was

born designed that
organ grounding new
mingling of tone—

That Was The
Week That Was
mothers too generous

their first born
had to be
sons ("unhurt" Michel)

Forty years gone
suddenly a taste
for Eyquem ("de" Montaigne)

at twenty put
off by his
polish not seeing

it essáys or
guessed an outgoing
modesty one's own

restless (not restive)
"aristocrat" desiring "laziness"
unprided desire—end (?)

Friends—all gone
with one with
many so-called

in one's "studies"
in age—old
as the news—

loved Catullus, sieur?
'Never Middling Poets
over your publisher's

door, every man
has the right
to fool himself

otherwise,' but will
you not add,
Michel, in that

too? 'Reading's profitable
pleasure—not much—
attracts judgment to

task I'll not
remember rather'll fire
my mind than

furnish it—song
does not work
my judgment, dazzles

my clear look
(luck?)—if not
the weight of

what I write
perhaps its intricacy—
o you'll regret

I pothered but
you'll have bothered'
Catullus played Bach

your place so
clean Bill said
you could eat

off the floor
I wouldn't suggest
it, stopped him

genetics sometimes Prorsus
Latin goddess of
births head first

whence *prose*—news?
Europe's sink before
art of sinking

'The Republic Plato
sought the course
of human events'

Vico doubling Bickerstaff
'Socrates the wisest
of uninspired mortal's

Struldbruggs Hamilton's *Manufactures*
That Was The
Week That Was

Each disenchanted Nazi
acted Polonius or
Wiggle & Failum

with noble prize
address I would
be Iago too

all things shall
be well now
we've put money

in your purse,
contact's skintight between
nations, long hot

summer "a coasted
torn-muffin" negro ghettos
police "horse," black

as white's, white
as black's cache—

mine tipples, dynamite's
in Hazard, Kentucky
which speaks Chaucer

'Gave sheep's brains
to Academician Lavrentyev'
—But Academician (stop)

has brains? 'Enough
to know he
can use more'

The victims of
looting the usual
excuse "jewish storekeepers"

Floats eats and
sings Gagarin (Wild Duck)
'I see the

earth .. visibility good
some space covered
by cumulus'—What's

it like up
there? 'The sky
is very, very

dark and the
earth is bluish.'
Elsewhere landing the

two astronauts inhaled
atomizers of wild
flowers, took showers

and sang 'Because
and not without
reason our poet

said *the best*
in life ends
with a song'

See
land,
flowers

Drink
hot
tea!

Promises .. brokers ..
as tho the
heart forcast: All

flown to th' moon,
I'm here parted
with everything, rare

rare, let snow
misgive these givings
and forsake misgivings

tiniest children play
their moons, rhomb,
so young *sensitif*

enharmonics, flyspeck
random crescendo their
aleatory. All a

Chinese sandwich—labors
a flatulence between
two pieces of

matzoh. *Died of*
triplets unable to
teach them to

speak three sounds
evenly—Paul H—
who'd planned four

stopped with the
second—in any
case not to

teach. Fly epistemologists—
can't pee dies.
Who's this Dios

whose focus
of his penis-
hand 4 or

5 inches from
his eyes makes
his center such

even his words'
worth interfuses in
that distance of

wide circle of
his john. One
word is too

often profaned since
Jefferson dined alone—
fooled, "history" integrates

lower limit body
upper limit dance,
lower limit dance

upper limit speech,
lower limit speech
upper limit music,

lower limit music
upper limit *mathémata*
swank for *things*

learned ("like" caged
"silence" which pulses)—
yet in each

case *what happens*—   .
Gracie Allen's dead
(*button up your*

overcoat) she who
acted the commuting
girl, business across

the threshold of
ma's parlor, telephoned
rightaway she'd arrived

safe (don't complain
Hollywood bought 12
copies of your

A Test) live
don't hope, all
one cantata, Bach's

one unposthumous. Expect
them to bathe?
—You don't mean

every fiscal year?
Old man looking
for some one

to endear (*Moon
Compasses*) premonition
of bonny prince

beheaded, 'poetry's of
the grief, politics
of the grievances'

No one to
speak to—red
grace of (near)

a shirt on
a child with
the feel of

autumn—a Jewish
boy I thought
gentile boys never

peed. Lonely the
season's quiet with
my love, terrace

cedar fence picket
our woods. Not
a false ending—

Job's, for which
the pious have
been blamed, restoration

of all he
had lost, indexed
in all its

affluence, tacking it
on to his
grievances too much

to take—'your
horse complex' (C.)
'what a preoccupation.'

—*that I so
carefully have dress'd
would he not*

*stumble? Forgiveness, horse
I was not
made a horse*

(the Prince of
the First Heaven
when he sees

the Prince of
the Second Heaven
dismounts) *even*

*with a thought
the rack dislimes
(grazing in a*

field, rubbed down
by other hands)
heels between two

*horses sees his
love, pure
kindness turn'd wild*

in nature dancing
as t'were (tethered
by reins

not frightened trampling
on the dead)
as true as

truest horse (capable)
music touch their
ears, eyes turn'd

modest gaӡe—
destroyed if changed
into a man—

unto thy value
I will mount
whose delight steps.

Our children's children
And you've arrived
A Vermeer blown

up into a
mural, a new
apartment house lobby

"partial" dentures, musical
drilling chance
Pitman, old

Ez 1962
1/29 in
The Times crossword

puzzle "Across/4
Pound, poet"
come-down to

99

a remove from
passions and noises
suffering together, simpler

alone, unurged horses,
or you forget
they are horses—

Holy Thursday (coincidence)
April 11, 1963
Pacem in Terris

"To *all* men—?
(today, my father,
13 years

ago) perhaps a
sign of peace
if Iván jokes

'In fallout
shroud yourselves calmly
walk, avoid panic'

Will *who* care
for his fools—
is He a

fool? from fountain
to wisdom, wisdom's
no fountain. Nothing

old to lose
by jetting.
I've counted words,

selected all my
life. An idiot
does not know

his loss. Not
wish you well
with the wind

tunnel? (Schönberg seems
lately to plait
song near Mozart)

your broken-glass painting
of last night's
universe is already

unfashionable—chorál out
of random input.

The voice of
episcopal goldwasser Polyuria
"to strip the

amour off the
enemy. Lucretius re-
wombs, he said,

when the earth
was young it
was able to

bare man and
feed him a
milk like substance,

as the earth
grew older she
could no longer

bare man, so
he had to
reproduce himself—the

industry of education
newtrons" In not
looking for metaphor

our worlds do
fly together: if
there are not

too many words.
Eloquence: self-laud.
My persistence reminds:

an escaped cat
ran down three
flights of stairs,

a little boy
after, he caught
it and climbed

back up the
three flights and
before closing the

door on it,
stroked it, 'you
pussy stay upstairs,

now *I'll* go
downstairs.' It became
the family joke—

'preventing an animal
errand.' They wash
the streets with

it in Poitiers.
Out of that
jakes my "Cats"

chaste—eyeing passionate
Italian lips two
thousand years near

to sharp them
and flat them
not in prurience—

of their voice—
eyes of Egyptian
deity that follow

each half step
blueing to translucent
Lunaria annua honesty

this side the
moon's. *Good Master*
Mustardseed I desire

you more acquaintance.
On a single
instrument runs to

chords, chords into
runs, broken homonyms
an empire silenced,

Sir Horse—a
daylight turned starred
heaven until it

dawns (after too
many hours) the
adjective had prepared

across many rays
for the noun.
Two alone, and

no syntax worth
a stop watch
for your ear

lobe—*dulce mihist*
kiss me last—
pietate mea—

my piety may.

Mr. Dooley: "th'
Bible an' Shakspere"
"D'ye read thim

all th' Time?"
"I niver read
thim, I use

thim f'r purposes
iv definse. I have
niver read them,

but I'll niver
read annything else
till I have

read thim. They
shtand between me
an' all modhren

lithrachoor." A Fulton
street market of
fish. I have

exchanged 10 books
I won't need
(how else *afforded*)

for The Book
Of the Dead
(not wished for

facsimile of papyrus
"whites, yellows, blues
greens—red and

yellow, yellow and
orange borders") *Pert-
em-hru* (pronounced

it how?) Praise
Coming forth by
day *on* earth

Returned everyday pérfect.
Mind you, heart,
strong. "Explained .. various

ways" *footnote Budge.
Kuh—voice that
did not scribe

passing, I cannot
budge to Budge.
Honesty *for* us

grave the
black glyphs
new moon

adz
(sail?)—
bird—
lamp
(cruse?)—
gaze

(mouth?)—
exult
tally,
wiggle
exult
tally—
(one:
three)
Sun
eye

15

An
  hinny
by
  stallion
out of
  she-ass

He neigh ha lie low h'who y'he gall mood
So roar cruel hire
Lo to achieve an eye leer rot off
Mass th'lo low o loam echo
How deal me many coeval yammer
Naked on face of white rock—sea.
Then I said: Liveforever my nest
Is arable hymn
Shore she root to water
Dew anew to branch.

Wind: Yahweh at Iyyob
Mien His roar 'Why yammer
Measly make short hates oh
By milling bleat doubt?
Eye sore gnaw key heaver haul its core
Weigh as I lug where hide any?
If you—had you towed beside the roots?
How goad Him—you'd do it by now—
My sum My made day a key to daw?
O Me not there allheal—a cave.

All mouth deny hot bough?
O Me you're raw—Heaven pinned Dawn stars
Brine I heard choir and weigh by care—
Why your ear would call by now Elohim:

Where was soak—bid lot tie in hum—
How would you have known to hum
How would you all oats rose snow lay
Assáy how'd a rock light rollick ore
Had the rush in you curb, ah bay,
Bay the shophar yammer *heigh horse*'

Wind: Yahweh at Iyyob 'Why yammer,'
Wind: Iyyob at Yahweh, 'Why yammer
How cold the mouth achieved echo.'
Wind: Yahweh at Iyyob 'Why yammer
Ha neigh now behēmoth and share I see see your make
Giddy pair—stones—whose rages go
Weigh raw all gay where how spill lay who'
Wind: Iyyob
'Rain without sun hated? *hurt no one*
In two we shadow, how hide any.'

The traffic below,
sound of it a wind
eleven stories
below: *The Parkway*
no parking there ever:
the deaths as
after it might be said
"ordered," the one
the two old
songsters would not
live to see—
the death of
the young man,
who had possibly
alleviated
the death of
the oldest
vagrantly back he
might have thought
from vying culturally
with the Russian
Puritan Bear—

to vagary of
Bear hug and King
Charles losing his head—
and the other
a decade younger
never international
emissary
at least not
for his President,
aged in a suburb
dying maundering
the language—
American—impatient now
sometimes extreme clarity—
to hurry
his compost
to the hill
his grave—
(distance
   a gastank)

he would
miss
living thru the
assassination

were it forecast to him
the dying face
would look quizzical?

'In another week,
another month
another—
I shall be driven,
how shall
I look
at this sign
then—
how shall

I read
those letters
then—
that's a thing
to remember—
I should
like to remember
this—
how shall
I look
at it,
then'

Like, after all:
and as I know
failing eyes
imagine,
as shortly after
his mother died,
walking
with me
to my class
thru the swinging
red leather doors
of the Institute
he remarked on
a small square pane
of glass in each of them,
there to prevent
if students looked
those going out
and those going in
from swinging the doors
into so to speak
mutual faces,
when I pleaded blindness
'I've walked thru
some years now
and never till you
said saw these panes'

he consoled with
'mere chance
that I looked'

But the death—
years later
of the young man—
he did not live thru
(no *Drum Taps*
no *Memories*
as for Walt)

that the teacher
overhearing
a student
thought a stupid jest—
the class
shocked into a "holiday"

Flown back from Love Field, Dallas
love—so—divided—
the kittenish face
the paragon of fashion
widowed
with blood soaked stocking
beneath the wounded head
she held in her lap—
Até
crazier than ever
infatuation of history
steps on men's heads—
flown back from Love Field, Dallas
as in *Kings* 'dalas'
the poorest,
we had all,
the "English" teaching drudge
with a holiday on his hands
from "papers"
a time for
to atone for your souls

the nation
a world
mourned
three days in
dark and in
daylight
glued to
TV
grieved as a family
the Kennedy's were a family—
Castro 'We should comprehend it
who repudiate assassination
a man is small
and relative in society
his death no joy'
not the joy of the Irish
a few weeks back
greeting their Parliament,
its actual house
the old Fitzgerald seat,
when the Boston Irish American President
on tour recalled
on his mother's side
his ancestral prototype who had left it
to write his own mother
from Paris
'that the seat of the Fitzgeralds
was not
conducive to serious thinking.'

Potentates (nominally)
dignitaries
cardinals
the military
mounted
and the horses
led the
tone

in politics

who's honest
true
to
death?
the off the cuff
opponent (Guildencrantz)
who'd stopped husking
for the nomination
until after the funeral
and after the funeral
forgot any day before
while conserving *Freedom*
nevermind *Liberty*—
honest—

the young dead's
great slip—
(pricing steel)
the twenty-third of April
only seven months laid (a
garland
for Shakespeare's birthday)
'My father always
told me
all business men
were sons-of-bitches.
I never
believed it
till now'

or Vietnam's witch
despising
Buddhists'
human wicks
with sympathies
for Western
First Lady
widow to widow
(Queen Margaret and dying Edward's queen)

And see another as I see thee now
could mourning soften

Eloquence
words of
a senator's eulogy
da capo five times:
'In a moment it was no more.
And so she took a ring
from her finger and placed it
in his hands'
And he added the fifth time:
'and kissed him and closed
the lid of the coffin.'

'Bethink you
if Bach's feet deserved such bounty
what gift must the Prince have offered
to reward his hands'
Capella, *alpha* in Auriga, little first goat
early evening early autumn
driven before them—west—
fall stars of evening

or Vesper there
Vesper Olympus dig air
court orchestra of uniformed Haiduks
habit Bach himself wore
"concertmaster" of four string players
his income not generous
'Friedmann, shall we go
over to Dresden to hear pretty tunes'
Italy's arias Händel's successes

one hundred four pages
of Frescobaldi's *Musical Flowers*
to copy, paper the fringe benefit from the Duke,
or pupil Ziegler to remember
in playing a hymn
melody is not alone

speaking the words thru it
a rare banquet in cypress
orange almond and myrtle
fragrance to turn a winter's evening to summer

or the court company of comedians
whose dispersal synchronized with Bach's arrival
not 'useful to accept a post
poorer than the one he abandons'
finger exercises traceries little pieces of himself
played over, saying 'That's how it ought to go'
no searching over the keyboard better silent
if there's nothing, until parts
speak to their fellows, true counterpoint
variety free thru consistency
later Orpheuses, Arions

Weimar not a street perpetuates his name
where Lucas Cranach lived and some say
Bach in Herder's house
more certain he was arrested
for urging his own departure—
They perpetuate the young dead's name with place
statesman stumping *The Tabernacle*, Salt Lake City
quick with his story of the first step
of a journey of a thousand years
in behalf
of the Test Ban Treaty, all journeys must
begin with a first step

(not counting on 42 days
to the unexpected grave)
'not to our size, but to our spirit'

And 'because' *alive* 'he knew the midnight
as well as the high noon'
the travellers stood chilling
to a parade of the first step

of might be that Chinese sage a thousand
years out of counting
a little more than a half-moon, dusk
a burial
poet old enough
to write it old enough history
like the horse who took part in it
shying from it, balking
despite himself

The fetlocks ankles of a ballerina
'Black Jack' Sardar with black-
hilted sword black dangled in silver scabbard from
the saddle riderless rider
his life looked back
into silver stirrups and the
reversed boots in them.
Finally a valentine
before his death
had he asked for it
I should have inscribed to him,
After reading, a song
for his death
after I had read at Adams House

John to John-John to Johnson

so the nation grieved
each as for someone in his or her family
we want Kennedy—
and the stock market fell and rose
on the fourth day
holy holy tetraktys
of the Pythagorean eternal flowing creation
and again without the senses TV
went back to its commercials
boots reversed flapping backward
and in another month
brought back the Indian's summer
'I was dreaming a high hole in rock

from which flowed the Seine
because that was how it looked
and was showing my father
of whom I rarely dream back to
its source when the doorbell
rang (the letter carrier, shocked sleep)
but your sheepsilver was here
a chunk of a summer's
Muscovy glass from the new film
The Glass Mountain'
almost Xmas—
and in less than another year
after 2000 years (a few less)
the dead's church
remembered not a moment too soon
to absolve the Jews of Yēshūa's (ah Jesu's)
cross—except for salvation

a smiling Gibbon's ground bass of a footnote
'spare them the pains of thinking'—
under the aspic of eternity
with the udder hand milking
the great Cow of Heaven—
Birjand, October five thousand nine hundred eleven
    (an anagram)
'hawking with the Amir (like old Briton)
a covey of see-see, the little partridge rose
with a whistle disappeared round a bend
the falconer leading held on gloved hand
by thong to a leg-ring the bright hawk
not hooded straining for release
which came shortly—rose
and brought the see-see to earth
the hawk poised on the quarry
claws gripped its neck
plucking the feathers: the falconer came up
took the neck of the living see-see
with the left hand and its legs in his right
and with one pull dismembered it
and gave the legs to the waiting hawk.'

He could not think another
thing that evening
simply a life
had stepped in in place of theory. Then love, young Isaac
burning for Rebecca, a comfort
not all and scorned in Augustine.

Eros agh nick hot hay mock on Eros us inked massy
    pipped eyes
now on th'heyday caught as thus mown

Dunk for the teeth that have rotted
(bread) soaked crust bare gums
glad car and cur bore the brunt of it
Woe woman woo woman
the fourth kingdom shall be as strong as iron
forasmuch as iron breaketh in pieces and
    subdueth all things
'perpetual violation of justice
.. maintained by .. political virtues
of prudence and courage ..
the rise of a city .. swelled into .. empire ..
may deserve .. reflection of .. philosophic mind
.. decline of Rome .. the
effect of immoderate greatness.
Prosperity ripened .. decay;
the causes of destruction multiplied with
    the extent of conquest,
and as soon as time or accident had removed
the artificial supports, the stupendous fabric
yielded to the pressure of its own weight ..
instead of inquiring
why the Roman empire was destroyed ..
should rather be surprised
.. it had subsisted so long.
The victorious legions, who, in distant wars,
acquired the vices of strangers and mercenaries,
first oppressed the freedom of the republic, and
afterwards violated .. the purple ..
emperors, anxious for .. personal safety

and .. public peace .. reduced to the
expedient of corrupting the discipline
.. and the Roman world was overwhelmed by a
deluge of barbarians ..
vain emulation of luxury, not of merit ..
Extreme distress, which unites the virtue
of a free people, embitters .. factions ..
As the happiness of a *future* life
is the great object of religion
we may hear without surprise
or scandal
that .. at least the abuse of Christianity
had some influence on the decline
and fall of the Roman empire. ·
The clergy successfully
preached the doctrines of patience and pusillanimity;
the active virtues of society were discouraged;
and the last remains of military
spirit were buried in the cloister:
a large portion of public and
private wealth .. consecrated .. charity and devotion;
and .. soldiers' pay .. lavished on useless
multitudes of both sexes who could only plead
the merits of abstinence and chastity ..
diverted from camps to synods ..
and the persecuted sects became
the secret enemies of their country ..
sacred indolence of monks was
devoutly embraced by a servile and effeminate age ..
Religious precepts are easily obeyed
which indulge and sanctify
the natural inclinations of their votaries ..
but the pure .. influence of Christianity
may be traced in its beneficial, though imperfect,
effects on the barbarian proselytes ..
This awful revolution may be
usefully applied to the instruction of the present
age .. The savage nations of the globe are the
common enemies of civilised society; and
we may inquire .. whether Europe is still

threatened with a repetition
of those calamities which formerly oppressed
the arms and institutions of Rome.
.. poor, voracious, and turbulent;
bold in arms and impatient
to ravish the fruits of industry .. The barbarian world
was agitated by the rapid impulse of war ..
the peace of Gaul or Italy was shaken
by the distant revolutions of China. ..
Cold, poverty, and a life of danger and fatigue
fortify the strength and courage of barbarians.
In every age .. oppressed
China, India and Persia,
who neglected, and still neglect
to counterbalance these natural powers
by the resources of military art ..
to command air and fire.
Mathematics, chemistry, mechanics,
architecture have been applied to the service of war;
and the adverse parties oppose to each other
the most elaborate modes of attack and defence.
Historians may indignantly observe
that the preparations of a siege
would found and maintain a flourishing colony;
yet we cannot be displeased that the
    subversion of a city
should be a work of cost and difficulty;
 or that an industrious people
should be protected by those arts
which survive and supply the decay of military virtue ..
Europe is secure from any future irruption
of barbarians; since before they can conquer,
they must cease to be barbarous. ..
Should these speculations be found doubtful
or fallacious, there still remains a more
humble source of comfort and hope. ..
no people, unless the face of nature
is changed, will relapse into their original barbarism.
The improvements of society
may be viewed under a threefold aspect.

1. The poet or philosopher illustrates his age and
country by the efforts of a *single* mind;
but these superior powers of reason or fancy
are rare and spontaneous productions;
and the genius of Homer .. or Newton
would excite less admiration
if they could be created
by the will of .. a preceptor.
2. The benefits of law and policy of trade
and manufactures, of arts and sciences
are more solid and permanent;
and *many* individuals may be qualified,
by education and discipline,
to promote, in their respective stations,
the interest of the community.
But this general order is the effect of skill and labour;
and the complex machinery may be decayed by time,
or injured by violence.
3. Fortunately for mankind,
the more useful, or at least more necessary arts,
can be performed without superior talents
or national subordination;
without the powers of *one*,
or the union of the *many*.
Private genius and public industry may be extirpated ..
But the scythe, the invention
or emblem of Saturn,
still continued annually to mow
the harvests of Italy;
and the human feasts of the Laestrigons
have never been renewed
on the coast of Campania.'

No lady Rich is very poor
No, laid o rich is very poor

kneecheewoe—
marriageable
the first lady astronaut

returning to earth
bruised her nose.

The wives of the poets
flew higher.
And to show for it—
on the hill near town the little cemetery
that would be seen from the Erie?
—No eulogies, Louis,
no.
Perhaps to see where his friend's song
not too clear while one led his own
would *button into the*
rest of it
the life of the fugue of it
not come to talk
at the funeral.
The dog as the old friend lay dead
would not cross his threshold
he was not there anymore
his room not his room
what was there not
for the day to go into—
the estuary up the river—
later thruout the house he ruled
while the others were interring him
the friend left at home in it
hearing the other voice as *then*
'you have never
asked anyone anything'

and Nestor, 'Odysseus—where
did you get those horses
I have never set eyes on
horses like these'
and he who with his wife
deceived even pride as she suffered
'it is easy *for a god*
to bestow even better horses
than these'

.. bathed
and sat down to dine
ate thought
.. o poor .. away from all baths ..
Hecuba with bare breast
she once fed him
wailing,
and for still another—
Thetis
and the nymphs
Glaukë and Thaleia and Kumodokë
Nesaië and Speio, Thoë, Halië
Kumothoë and Actaië and Limnoreia
Melitë, Iaira, Amphitoë and Agauë
Doto and Proto, Pherousa and Dunamenë
Dexamenë and Amphinomë and Kallianeira
Doris and Panopë, Galateia
Nemertes and Apseudes and Kallianassa
Klumenë and Ianeira and Ianassa
Maira and Oreithuya and Amatheia
of the deepest bath

negritude no nearer or further
than the African violet
not deferred to
or if white, Job
white pods of *honesty*
satinflower

16

An

inequality

wind flower

17

A CORONAL
for Floss

Anemones

> "But we ran ahead of it all ...
> Anemones sprang where she pressed
> and cresses
> stood green in the slender source—
> And new books of poetry
> will be written ... "

1928   Not boiling to put pen to paper
Perhaps a few things to remember— ...
"I heard him agonizing,
I saw him *inside*" ...

                   "*A*"–1

    ... art's high effort
    vying with the sun's heat

    shadows small—
    when rather like thick peasants

    out of Brueghel
    after working

    you stretch out—
    the sun among

    the hayricks of Its fields
    and artless find time.

             Poem 26 from *55 Poems*

1930 The melody! the rest is accessory:

    My one voice. My other: is
    An objective—rays of the object brought to a focus,
    An objective—nature as creator—desire
      for what is objectively perfect
    Inextricably the direction of historic and
        contemporary particulars.
                "A"–6

In a work most indigenously of these States, and beginning perhaps a
century of writing, as Wordsworth's preface of 1800 began it in England,
in *Spring and All* (1923) William Carlos Williams writes:
Crude symbolism is to associate emotions with natural phenomena,
such as anger with lightning, flowers with love; it goes further and
associates certain textures with ... It is typified by the use of the word
"like" or that "evocation" of the "image" which served us for a time.
Its abuse is apparent. The insignificant "image" may be "evoked" never
so ably and still mean nothing.
            Sincerity and Objectification

 ... The principle of varying the stress of a regular meter and counting
the same number of syllables to the line ... transferred from 'traditional'
to cadenced verse ... in *Spring and All*: not that [Williams] made each
line of a stanza or printed division carry absolutely the same number of
syllables— ... but there seems to have been a decided awareness of the
printed, as well as the quantitative, looseness of vers libre. Obviously,
what counts is quantity; print only emphasizes—yet, printing correctly,
a poet (Williams or Cummings) shows his salutary gift of quantity ...
one who has vicariously written, rather than painted as he has always
wished to do ... conscious of his own needs through the destruction of
the various isolated around him ...
           American Poetry 1920–1930

1931   WILLIAM CARLOS WILLIAMS
        MARCH
      An "Objectivists" Anthology pp. 196–200

1933   "who has
       a
        taste

            "for something
                        that will
                                    warm
                                                up"

            snow
                        for
                                    my friend's birthday
                        ...
            "and
                        so
                                    on."
                                                Song—3/4 time from *55 Poems*

1934   *names are sequent to the things named*
                                    ...

            Is the poem then, a sestina
            Or not a sestina?

            The word sestina has been
            Taken out of the original title. It is no use
                                                (killing oneself?)

                        —Our world will not stand it,
                        the implications of a too regular form.

            Hard to convince even one likely to show interest
                                                in the matter
            That this regularity to which 'write it up' means
                                                not a damn ...
            If it came back immediately as the only
            Form that will include the most pertinent subject
                                                of our day— ...
            Cannot mean merely implied comparison, unreality
            Usually interpreted as falsity ...

            The mantis might have heaped up upon itself a
            Grave of verse,
            But the facts are not a symbol ...

No human being wishes to become
An insect for the sake of a symbol.

"*Mantis*," *An Interpretation* from *55 Poems*

1935 1869. A Chapter of Erie. C. F. Adams (Jr.) ...
Collected at the Erie Station in Jersey City,
(Ribbed Gothic and grilled iron)

"*A*"–8

1936 The white chickens of 24b are even more gentle than the mosaic
cok (24a) descended of gentility ... It may take only four words
to shift the level at which emotion is held from neatness of surface
to comprehension...

A Test of Poetry

1940 They were together now in the time when the Aztec calendar
was correct and the Old World calendar of that period in error.
No hands of a clock crossed the figures of hours. There was less
difference between them than between the Americans and her.
She had planted a sprig of Creeping Charlie—her eyes like stars
moving— and was oblivious as to whether it was called Wandering
Jew or a weed ... The film was running again: something not
advertised on the billboard ... highly original and yet disjunct ...
something about Columbus ... La Niña. The title translated: the
girl. And continued: Columbus on his first return voyage entering
the harbor of Palos. Suddenly the little theatre went dark ... he
drove on ... a street from which he could see the steps going up
to the columns of the porch of the Capitol—not much more than
a hundred years old.

"*Ferdinand*" from *It was*

1942 If number, measure and weighing
Be taken away from any art,
That which remains will not be much:—

Poem 14 from *Anew*

1943 You three:—

Poem 42 from *Anew*

" ... this poem, all Z's art, that is to say,
his life ..."

W

1944   William Carlos Williams
THE WEDGE
[to] L.Z.

1946   "Dr. W. C. Williams
9 Ridge Road
Rutherford, N.J.

5/22/46

Dear Celia:
        Keep it if you like. Could music
be made for it?

Best

Bill

enc.: *Choral: The Pink Church*."
(music written June 1946)
to Williams—
       ... all gentleness and its
enduring ...
      "Poetry For My Son When He Can Read"
           from *5 Statements for Poetry*

"Dear Louis:
  This is the longest labor at which I was ever the attendant.
But here it is. Such as it is.

As ever,

Bill

6/4/46"
(inscription in *PATERSON* (*Book One*)

1948   Aristotle knew that "the argument of the *Odyssey* is not a long
one." And Chapman spurred by the job of rendering summed it
up as "A man," or perhaps just "man." The friendliest reader for
the time being forgets, still scampering through Williams. ... the
horse of man's "whole grasp of feeling and knowledge in the
world." ... (and we are in *Paterson's* time) and his Stein-ish
definition of substance "a this."

An Old Note on WCW

Dear Louis:

Happy Birthday (my own); what's the different? Thought you might enjoy the enclosed greeting.

Maybe Celia will set it to music—notice the slow nostalgic line.

Best

Bill"

(enc.: "Turkey in the Straw")

"Tuesday [Sept.]

Dear Celia:

No, I guess I didn't exactly mean the same tune as Turkey in the Straw—but after that nature ...

Best

Bill"

(music written 10/6/48)

1949

W

Ah, my craft, it is as Homer says:
"A soothsayer, a doctor, a singer
and a craftsman is sure of welcome
where he goes." Never
have I seen anything like you,
man or woman.
I wonder looking at you.
Well, in Delos
once I saw something like you,
a young palm sprung at Apollo's altar,
I've been even that far—along
with others and their raft of trouble.
Seeing that sapling I was stunned
for no other tree like it grows out of the earth.
And yet I wonder and am stunned—
you might be that girl—
at the thought of touching your knees.

"III, Chloride of Lime and
Charcoal" from Some Time

1954   William
                 Carlos
                 Williams

                   alive!

              thinking of
              Billy

The kid
shoots
to
kill,

But to
the expanse
of his
mind

who heard
that word
before,

scape
of a
letter

soars
with the
rest of
the letter

gulled by
the kid's
self-sacrifice:

reach
C
a cove—
call it
Carlos:

smell W
double U
two W's,
ravine and
runnel:

these
sink
high

in
high
fog

which
as
it
lifts,

the other
world
is
there:

the sight
moves—

open—

soothes

smoothes
over

the
same word

that
may have,
to touch,

two faces—
the heart
sees into—
of one
sound:

the
kid
's torn,
shot

so quickly
it sounds
water:

purls

a
high
voice

as with
a lien
on
the sky

that becomes

low now
frankly

water—

called also—

softly—

a kill.

That song
   is the kiss
it keeps
   is it

The
   unsaid worry
for what
   should last.

By the intimacy
   of eyes,
or its inverse—
   restiveness

Of heart—

      ...

The gold that shines
   in the dark
of Galla Placidia,
   the gold in the

Round vault rug of stone
   that shows its
pattern as well as the stars
   my love might want on her floor

The quiet better than crying
   peacock is immortal
she loves, knows
   it so pretty

That pretty in
   itself is enough
to love.

            "4 Other Countries" from
               Barely and widely

Passer, deliciae meae puellae
        Sparrow, my girl's pleasure, delight of my girl,
        a thing to delude her, her secret darling
        whom she offers her fingernail to peck at,
        teasing unremittingly your sharp bite,
        when desire overcomes her, shining with love
        my dear, I do not know what longing takes her,
        I think, it is the crest of passion quieted
        gives way to this small solace against sorrow,
        could I but lose myself with you as she does,
        breathe with a light heart, be rid of these cares!
                                            "Catullus II"

                                                        5/20/58
        Dear Bill,
            This is, as you will find out, for the nation ...
                                            Yours,
                                            Louis
        [anticipating *PATERSON* (*Book Five*) and his 75th birth-
        day]

1960   (In Karel van Mander's painting of two Englishmen playing chess
        —William Carlos Williams is not against thinking they are
        Shakespeare and Ben Jonson painted from life, 1606—"Shake-
        speare's" lowered but seeing eyes and red affectionate lips are
        absorbed by the chess move of his hand; "Ben's" open eyes stare
        blindly from a coarse face; the literal sense of the painter suggests
        the identity of his models.)

                            ...

        "the living tongue resembled that tree which father Huc saw in
        Tartary, whose leaves were languaged ... mated by new shoots
        and leafage of expression ... "—as good for thought as Williams'
        The Botticellian Trees

                            ...

        "—they had eyes ..
                —and saw,
        saw with their proper eyes ..

which is she whom I see
    and not touch her flesh?"

Grand entr'oeil, et regard joly
                     Bottom: on Shakespeare

1962   Pretty
Look down out how pretty
the street's trees' evening green
with the day's with them
on globular lights no Hesperides
was has fruit more lemony
orangey cherryie honeydew melon white
like several white sports cars
turned the corner no peachier
headlights blaze in dark sides
of a row of cars
half-parked on the sidewalk
while for once nowhere here
fruits smell sing the mechanics
                     from *After I's*

Ille mi par esse deo videtur
He'll hie me, par *is* he? the God divide her,
he'll hie, see fastest, superior deity,
quiz—sitting adverse identity—mate, in-
        spect it and audit—
you'll care ridden then, misery hold omens,
air rip the senses from me; now you smile to
me—Lesbia's aspect—no life is to spare me
        [voice hoarse in a throat]
linked tongue set torpid, tenuous support a-
flame a day mown down, sound tone sopped up in its
tinkling, in ears hearing, twin eyes tug under
        luminous—a night.   "Catullus LI"

Williams' inscription in L.Z.'s copy of *Pictures from Brueghel*

135

18

An unearthing
my valentine
if I say it now will
it always be said.
I always know
it is I who have died
yet in that state

sorrow for you
by yourself.
Thinking of you
without me
without years
of hours
that time is.
Selfish of
me to wish you
to merely
live long

to fulfill
no time
where your
thought for
me has no sense
for with
that thought
it is I have died.
I mean don't cry
in that sense
I cannot now

get around
thinking I am dead
where with you
now I have no place
as I say
it now
and you sense
it always said.

I am here let the days live their
lines two days bird's down blown on wire
mesh fence jot down assures life a note(book).
who won't sense upper case anymore: iyyob (jōb)
swift would have known sobbing it every birthday
yovad yom yahweh the surgeon a surge on
tall as the mast a nipponese liner rising
sun on the flag of a high mast
sails after the week in port into a
seeled fog of sunset east having come west
going home. *typee* tattoo the water woven as
the surgeon operated on another wound offhand saw
the mentula tattooed SWAN remarked later with the
sailor's recovery *how charming how apt* and the
buoy confused exclaimed SWAN? *that was SASKATCHEWAN.*
or found in the debris of the acropolis
a long lost right leg (wisdom?) athene's parthenon
pediment.
                    forgive: I don't recall names: rote.

Stupid perhaps bright with the youngest of my
days for you more than my work nobody
to speak of did it say a wedding
rite sang not vain chance I Sent Thee Late
'Not Exactly Personal C.Z. wanted to save
this poem written in 1922. "I sent thee
late"—wanting one supposes honor, a "rosy" (?)
"wreathe" asks that it "breathe" of "thee" even
if it is "itself"

137

Vast, tremulous;
Grave on grave of water-grave:

Past.

Futurity no more than duration
Of a wave's rise, fall, rebound
Against the shingles, in ever repeated mutation
Of emptied returning sound.'

Death not lived thru *big a sweeter fig*
a greek gathering of early flowers that may
happen if they come out notes that happened
but not co-star cluster again *For a Thing*
by Bach tho I read as she sees
such Life as is Our God .. if like
to errant stars .. of Thy source .. as to
the immortelle long after the gathering is given
give .. measureless .. still increate. These fallen petals now
the rest let be our lives do not
yet know enough shall at 90 and 81.

Weep—rather others. world's a huge thing. half
asleep. e.e.c. as young man saw
an old man 3/3 dead. if one
third seems wandered for 2 left alone figure
6/3? the little girl 4-year old
asked to meet the great man did not want
to 'I have already met enough people.' all
their world's done to change the world is
to make it more ugly to the airport.

When they use elbow or arm boards to
cover the whole keyboard fast rather than their
fingers spanning octave to octave they fly to
lunes together and the epicene stentorian drops
bass lower than his stones we're to watch see.
The young o young-eyed pitiful cannot bear that
gnawing pain sorrow sorrow and 'the music saves

it' I may not ever translate it precisely
carried having enough its hoving over. THRONGS OF
VIETNAMESE PILGRIMS VISIT POND OF MIRACULOUS FISH.
'The pond is in Quang Nam about 30
miles west of Danang where hate between Buddhists
(about 80 per cent of the population) and
Roman Catholics equals "*strong*." The miracle happened about
two months ago in the middle of the crisis
the Buddhists accusing the Government of discriminating against
them. Word spread. A giant fish apparently a
carp swimming in a pond the incarnate Buddha.
The fish was so big and could be
seen so easily it was attracting the attention
of the villagers. From all over the province
Vietnamese came to the pond to be its
fish. At this point the district chief a
newly shrived Catholic told American aide that the
"pilgrimage" was an act of opposition. American decided
to clean out *his* pond. With new troops
from Col. Le Quang Tung's special forces both
marched to that pond to *get* that fish.
Troops fired their automatic weapons into *their* pond.
They placed ten mines in said pond and
set them off. They blew up and killed
everything in that pond except the fish. He
came on swimming. They started feeding it bread
so to tempt him up to the surface.
They followed bread with hand grenades pitched into
the water twice. Twice terrific explosions twice the
fish officially "continued" to swim. *Ich hub dir
in bud* (Kentuckian for *jump in the lay-ake*
brother tongue too.) Other continents encroach' as
we can see by the belly-fanny dancing
of the tights over the buttocks of "our"
women the slim erectile trousers of "their" men.
Not that we digged original sin reading Gibbon's
"an useful scavenger" of a defender of persecution
who used saints for his history in support of
his arguments. Rather noted a statesman hump TV-
free face between a pumpkin and a shark.

139

For a roman à clef all resemblance to living or
dead obviously intended if these find their identities
in them. For the young starting out: better
ordure than order's arrogance of 'ideas' and 'ideals.'
We warm us may ah Lesbia what cue
may maim us the theatre marquees too big
to read, a friend writes 'the song preserves
recurring saves us' the song preserves a store's
preserves packed rancid: death wars' commonplace no hurt
wars not Old Glory's archaic even for MacArthur
'How many killings per Diem Phu on Nhu'
housewife alarmed veteran unpacking from the supermarket 'I
told him not to put the encyclopedia with
the vegetables, PENTHOUSE FLOOR send the elevator down.'

When I am dead in the empty ear
you might ask what was he like away
from home: on his job more patient with
others than himself more patient with strangers that's
always so: what if the song preserves us?
As *you* said stone sculpture's still and moves
and to intrigue us further the mobile moves
with its sustaining current the space is still:
which is less abstract solid or more sensed?
non-sense like the great thing is not
to refuse their "honor" best not "deserve" it
(N. 'they will *all* think they deserved it')
what work excepts or ends. fiddler and fiddle
together. *Man and Sheep: Odysseus with the Sacrifice:*
his kid's clothes sprawled over the stone, Pablo—
'art begs disrespect, calculators can only give answers.
Bad, good: horses or sheep in a field.'

No not an efficient man only an observant
sits down with an aspirin without a prayer
eight words a line for love: *y-eye, yigh*
pointed the kid, *y-eyes* intentions blaze *light lights*:
an order out of hiatus joining a chain:
"*An*": faring no cause to an unowned end:
story of a fiddler from pogrom to program:

Doughty: 'the Semites are like to a man
sitting in a cloaca to the eyes and
whose brows touch heaven': but for his 'heaven'
the producer's offer to Schönberg Hollywood's 'infernal passion
terrestrial paradise and heaven' answered by, 'Then why
do you need *my* music': *Shahnamah* relegated to
tribesmen and dervishes, read aloud in encampments, chanted
striding in coffee houses: by my friend who
eats like a bird *da capo* a vulture:
stick whacks a statue, execration grave's my door:
Klamath floods: the old man of the creek
up high ground shored hearing voices under him
"out of his head" climbed awake 3 nights
72 hrs watching his house spirited away below
snows after weeks' rains bid to stay months:
and the nation's draft my window's: soldiers killed
in small *squirm*ishes (the newspaper's misprint): whose
the hernia of a book: that the devils
not be driven into swine or Jerusalem rabbinate
like the Curia kidnap a little scholar:
the weight of the wait: how many books
can a man read: man unkind womb unkind:
alter ego *jünger* ego: "reality" grammarian added an
ity: philosophize: if I cannot live their lives
for them, to write their costive posies is whose (?) "lie":
fool horse Sophi if these lines were broken
down into such jewelled shorts word for word
they might exceed The Decline and Fall of
the American Poem by six folios, when (if)
life is too much ineffable is *His* title:
the "I" can't get around "my" 'overcome by
undue sense of right': whistler: 'no desire to
teach the rare few who had early rid
themselves of the clap claque of a public:
in the Jews quarter in Amsterdam he did
not lament that the gabardine was not Greek':
art she: occupied with her own counterpoint coverlet
Father not guilty: Emanuel's 4 Angels with Hats
on their Heads: top hats tipped to a
tramp: the drawing Old Tacit never returned: as

we furnish anew stir recall half asleep *then*:
old song: now knowing-it (?) goes with it:
only the closest close keeps one awake: child
called Silence unsure ever when she was called
or shut up: old man and close lady
as one August gust on another stop speaking
in pretty ears: B's *Notenbuch* compiled by both:
her copy has her initial no other signature:
'between order and sensibility in its power at
once to suggest all complexity and keep every
form each form taking up the same theme':
not by "association" it is *so* things come to
me.

    Why "free"? They'd sing 'Horses, horses I'm
crazy about horses' Where Luvah doth renew *his*
brings *The Horses of Lu*, they "*A*"–*7* horses:
"Lou" (*her* voice) *my* name *God's my life*
forty years later The Adirondack Trust Company of
Saratoga (Drive-in Banking and F R E E Parking While Banking)
trust "Health—History—Horses" *He* has become as
talkative as Bottom a weaver and says for
me all that follows: 'we laugh at that elixir
that promises to prolong life to a thousand
years and with equal justice may be derided?
Who shall imagine that his dictionary can enbalm his
language, that it is in his power to
change sublunary nature. Sounds are too volatile for
legal restraints. To enchain syllables and to lash
the wind are equally undertakings of pride unwilling
to measure its desires by its strength. That
signs might be permanent . . like the things?
To explain requires the use of terms less
abstruse than that which is to be explained
and such terms cannot always be found. Words
hourly shifting, names have often many ideas, few
ideas many names. But every art is obscure
to those that have not learned (?) it. The
exuberance of words, to admit no testimony of
living authors, but when my heart in the
tenderness of friendship solicited admission for a favorite

name—to *per*sue perfection was like the first
inhabitants of Arcadia to *chace* the sun, which
when they had reached the hill where he
seemed to rest, was still beheld at some
distance from them: that I set limits to
my work which would in time be ended
tho not completed, that he whose design includes
whatever language can express must often speak of
what he does not understand: writes hurried by
eagerness to the end—that the *English Dictionary*
was written with little assistance of the learned,
and without any patronage of the great; not
in the soft obscurities of retirement, or under
the shelter of academic*k* bowers, but amidst inconvenience
and distraction, in sickness and in sorrow—success and
miscarriage .. empty sounds .. having little to fear
from censure or from praise.'
                                  Clear hand is C's
'Thou that do cover'—But whose then, her
son's words I of all life embrace, as T
answered echoing the ugly lady: if she or
the beautiful one fell into the sea which
would he dive for first: but Madam you
swim so well. L (who?) *'witness his hand'*
(as white of egg as of child conceived
not wisdom but starred tear furthered to achieve,
the thigh's slender not blind clock of history
remembers when the genitals hang higher than the
table chronicle began to shake bad) 'there is
a march of *science* but who shall beat
the drum for its retreat.' Her soft look
played, would not harm a fly, speech gentle
or he hold still 'seed-time till fire purge
nor let the sea surpass nor rain to drown
sleep hand in hand who to blot out.'
What we *would* preserve 'o'er the marish glides
to the subjected plain.' Napalm no palm, manroot
pollutes their throats, "eloquence" that is old Latin's
past participle merely declaims. Blood does not syllabicate
pulse. Pride false to its own voice lolling

143

snake eyes they could not find the artist
so they hung the picture so he walks
with Lincoln (who said of the preacher's sermons
'he got to writin 'em and was too
lazy to stop.' Twenty minutes to whittle one
peg, a big chair needs 30 to 90—
pegs, no nails unless asked by a customer—
the better part of a month starting with
cutting the tree for a rocker, people ain't
willin to pay what it's worth, they don't
understand how much time takes to make it:
or a chairmaker born in Poor Fork.) We
are nothing if not American. But we
are *not* a Europe-of-the-United States
an Asia-of-an Africa-of-a South America
-of-the-United States. Aware 'gathers ground fast'
how fast their empire dwindled, child 'tasted *A*'
(Hen Adams) *schlissel* to *key*, H.J. intensely in
New York the year that I was born.
60 gone, my son plays Ives 20 of
nostalgic homespun circles thru fiddle, "Proud?" well if
their praise means well. As if one root
went 1000 years deep flew back from Iceland
to round full cycle beginning Eric The Red.
Thank you, hell does not wish to be
fed anymore never wanting anything to write *about*.
All their ever never my never ever: let be.
Above children bumping heard *The Great Fugue*.
Goal's naturally breathless, look back, *an, a, the*—
praise or as you wish the reticence of
all my omissions, not "smarter" than Catullus, thank
you, he was Savage struck it "uncommon" and
who, Time, can plead Roman did not compel
complications, Celtiberia still Spain—dim to sum up
but that one horror dims another, I cannot
teach-in, sit-in, orgy-for nor will in obscurity malinger
for those competing to gag they needed me—
how ineffable such a small flatulence of the
intelligent and discriminating General Reader sounder than whose
Pew black or white competitively they're the same.

Heather and white candles were pretty, marron glacés
good, printed letterheads *would* be timesaving but late
expedience for kindness like the theologian's pastorate "two
Xians both Jews." Valé, fruitcake, volley, and (true)
cigs medicines certain tissue ought not be taxed
nature sure enough has taxed man's rump enough.
I see with the inflation boys march West
Less Land Ia Drang news one more less safer
hailstone General revealing only small losses, some the
inevitable fault of bombing his own men, 'but
we've stopped the little bastards VC's,' and
enlisted officer urged valor when Secretary Offense
shot off bulletproof mouth his hinny's teeth raising
the promise of 200,000 draftees. "The stupid war
in Viet Nam" afterthought of an earlier stupid
Frog's thought for Glory not all neat o.
Mac—gee! resigned for a "Cadillac" job the
TV announcer said it left his President's basement
for a jump from 28 to 70 thousand
to head a Foundation. The Ecumenical Council ended
signing peace? Unless a miracle, said Cyrus, rusk
(twice baked) never informed the people. Remorse said:
'*one* Senator—*imperialism*?I don't delight in semantics
the U.S. is guilty violating international law.'
Rock well all shut up if you don't
swallow my knuckles I'll knock out the few
remaining teeth Ours Total resort to maiden again?
'I understood whatever was unintelligible *would* be transcendental
.. Broadway .. pig .. only one ear .. parted the other
to vagrant dogs .. ' Dickens, old: *American Notes*. 'Bach
or the Devil' laughed as to mastery 'nothing
wonderful you merely strike the right note.' POWER
FAILURE EIGHT STATES: Achilles' Heel of American Giant.
New Yorkers kind in the blackout. Dark named cities.
Watts, Harlem. A cyclone from Arkansas gone northeast
with furniture, bedsprings bar billiard ping pong tables
cuspidors dressers that the Lord giveth over Massachusetts.
'Fond of listening to other players' the solution
of the up to date. *Life* thumbed—three
photographs: a monument to Lumumba his wax figure

in a glass booth; corpse of another year
salved from heaped plaster; 4 small Congolese boys
left to play alone hide-and-go-seek
a game of grasping the last stake standing
of an iron fence to swing out to
devastation that does not own them, happy in
their play: o son of the umbilical cord
of the Gemini capsule and *cryobiology* mere cold
does not kill (it is the *slow* freezing
of ice crystals that ruptures the cell)
superfast frozen suspended animate back to Sumeria's recipe
'Grind to a powder pear-tree wood, grind
with flower of the *moon* plant, then dissolve
it in beer and let the man drink.'
Would: wood:
                                    a massive operation with small results:
my love watched TV between Ti and Ki
danang cryochore intervention in santo domingo transcendental
                                                            neutrality
heard the astronauts would sleep if not urged
from the ground (old Lady Clio mutter 'ruination'
shamed by behind tho no one had followed
it seemed turning round ashamed 'had he followed?'
a young man 'since the last detonation' the
sailor who'd not reenlist defeat at dong xoai)
my love scorched as she watched the self-immolation
of roger allen la porte 5 a.m. at u.n.
(seminarian briefed chrystie street where I was born)
the quicked quaker norman morrison his own torch
in front of the pentagon, an older lady
whose name was hushed: only in my love's
room did her plants not burn: in world's
hangar great room *honesty* a shade gray
the unminded plant burned with all others where
white is at least as false as true
that fittest survives.
                                    Weeping: the food he eats.
The spirits would not return to rest under
the huts burnt to the ground their lifegiving
handful of rice smoke when the rice paddies

146

fired. The marine with the cigarette lighter did
not know nor the air cavalry bombing indiscriminately
cultured now like the innocent child shamed by
the pain his birth caused perverse burned hating all
males who impregnate. Here an old woman weeps
as in the Melanesian tale the old woman's
spirit crouched under the bedstead not known scalded
after the Harvest Tide when the dead return
for their Day then all but the longing spirit
return all the dead to return remembered only
in the next Harvest Tide the Year's Time
scalded unknown by the day's broth her daughter
spilled from a coconut cup weeps heard known
to 'I thought you were here only for
the one Day' weeps 'I shall go now'
known now cutting a coconut in half as
alive keeping the half with three eyes giving
her daughter the other 'I am giving you
the half that is blind tho you look you
will not see me I am taking the
half with the eyes and I shall see
you when I come back with the others.'
Trobrianders: born of these spirits *Baloma bogè isaika*
the baloma gave it of the father's way
with the child's into the womb they'll say
or know nothing: when the *Baloma* the dead
soul is old his teeth fall out his
skin's loose and wrinkled he goes to the
beach and bathes in salt water throws off
his skin like snake becomes child again a
waiwaia in *utero* (belly: cavity of earth) or
just born: baloma woman's there with a basket
or plaits coconut leaf to carry *waiwaia* to
Kiriwina village places it into the womb of
(that's later) its mother so she is *nasusuma*
pregnant: or the *waiwaia* go into the sea
hide in *popèwo* floating scum in washed on
stones *dukupi* or come along on large tree-
trunk *kaibilabala* or attach to dead leaves *libulibu*:
when wind and high tide blow plenty of

this stuff towards the shore girls are afraid
to bathe in the sea: while bathing may
feel a thing touch or hurt: sometimes cry
A fish has bitten me: th' *waiwaia* being inserted:
or in a dream *baloma* inserts the *waiwaia*.
As to your "cause" *U'ula* a mere share:
dripping water a finger may also—not man:
also the fatherless always *the baloma gave it*
tho the girl with *waiwaia* no father 's "no good"
gala taitala Cikopo'i where is no father no
man to take it in his arms.

My

sweet 9/3 wonder if I'm not you're 3
smile conjugate: 'I stumble you stumble Istanbul'
'as when an upright woman holds her scale
weight in one hand wool in the other
to earn a meager wage for her children'
I am my father reading to my mother
if not Isaac *iliad:* 'they live for memory:
with them in the sense that they think
of nothing else: the more in their past
the more find it': *Maud-Evelyn.* I read there
he plays here. 'So life hasn't seen anything?'
'Nothing.' 'Then he hasn't kept the things?'
'He has kept everything.' Paid: but not for
the work. This fable of life its face
like sudden night when nothing is said but
in 'silences that cause the thought to flow'
head splitting and not splitting: to think hair-
splitting: but swift recall softest hair and its
head presumably danced in the child feet: fireplace
with a window over it so he thought
to watch the flames reach up to snow.
Let The Hermit sing *I do not know*
whom Edan will sleep with but I don't
that fair Edan will not sleep alone. Let
the page turner look as if he earned
his Bach—Malbrook gone to war 'bribing neighbors
to fight their own quarrel .. amongst our enemies
our allies .. that extenuation he so much despised

men are but men .. who amused with bonfires .. '
Thankful crowded frozen then as valet and maid
truckers in his move as he drove the
white *Dart* with the youthful red upholstery: lake
cloud and maiden cloud Little Dipper flying ahead
of the windshield: of gratitude there is less
than happiness: the one odd moment of happiness
6/3 alone so near two each 1/3 chills alone:
bridge with three piers fog's of the water:
span not mirrored where three piers mist
sheaved waistlines reflected one and one and one.

'What nature delights in' says Savage 'the observer
on the level with the object: a shell
reversed no false ornament, moss and fern stuck
with root outward, a crystal sparkling at bottom
or top, loose soil or plashing water; rudeness
is here no blemish' the emasculated conception: 'A
man who hates children and dogs can't be
all male vicieuse.' Demolition: what fears of tears
their hateful deference water for mash: Hell
a *mood* (that hollow word!) His Friday's pun
Good but does not pass for that: an
opera's mournful wail 'Bye-Bye Brook-a-leen-a'
portent I shivered to as kid: a Sicilian
brass band blaring Brahms' march to the 6-foot blot
what Mad King pawn braiding his pubic hairs
Divine *comedy*. We'll move from our belongings disposed
of in a song '*Kwanon, sine qua non*'
how unhappy a place once blessed can grow
'Job's city of Kratz the second city of
Austria' C said. The metaphor barely a rhetor's
loveless word quickened only when the laugh's with
all we lived: afar brought to the fore.
Leave their years of drain as the seventh
decade comes offering the same insolence my patience
had built on drains drained arrogance drained spirit
drained authority ourari in their air conditioner.
Our *Pickaninny* painting looks civil rites behind her

'and what natural use have *cartons* of books'
heritage late come from the buffaloes with these
we can't stir before our coupling apartment hunters
who according to the clause of the lease
can come to look as it suits the
landlord: 'seeing 4 walls they've visions of empire.'
'Who cares.' That one who cared says that.

Has scion so much sheet music scores books
to which I have added to support the
live dead, the stone dead, the quick near
dead, the few to be alive dead—and
not for status? 'We have no wishes now.'

TV advertiser for stocks: "the one permanence change."
'Think my dear of Heraclitus' fee were he alive.'
There pressed to me my old father's soul
'Deign? no. nor detain reverence in his way,
keeping your days apart all one and filial
silence will stay the wait, lampposts of your
courting borough be a woods.' Then in myself
her look in an areaway said 'the spring's
one white crocus Eden no friends to share.

Never fear we'll be found in our city
smog ensuring medical costs four times your pay.'
80 odd dwellings burnt imagery of the poets
'the fashion to draw eyes like—but such
eyes you like no more than such noses
you came into the world with less, no
compliments, no presents, you disarm those whom a
note glances to remind of their conceits, who
when they envy think they create *mit fühlung*
aspirant relatives parasitically hugging genius to
                                        inhuman family:
be it but a line or a dot let it persist
at that solely with the unearthing crocus: by
this time Katsuhika Hokusai we are like you
only with the room on the corner of
Hell Street where we'll be rarely happy to

see you since you have passed that way.
Let the mad dogs' transports enjoy all success.
We are quiet where they cannot exist alone
and alone our desire won't shadow their living.'

With the fireworks of The Fourth at the
sill the black smudges of a child's white
first shoes show, a tin pie plate he
painted is Persian a little beyond the red
pipecleaner Valentine the bare the tiny has poise.
All-star-what-shade-blue-what-shade-blue?
The ashtray with the painted daisy its eye
on the tablemat near her, 'place what dear?'
If he dropped in it would be perfect.
A garden of shadows on the walls after
all eyes walls looking eyes see sun's greetings
your jungle of flower pots (a chest weighs
f-holes of spruce all or nothing) hang the
unbellied fiddle painted black inside with its black
cardboard shelves for—its monkey-like scroll, its
ebony pegs little arms—the little replica of
the "Ste. Maria" making it down trough, the
green and walnut cow: (trinkets) 'fetishes' Brancusi laughed
toying with his: black washrag folded over the
tile wall soap dish enough sculpture, an emptiness
mirrored, an animate instrument without vindictiveness.

20 years

you've wanted a bolster? the old chair pillow
folded in half tied by its gold strings,
small can serve also as a lady's muff
no one'll have seen anything like it, with one
puff a bolster, and as fulfillment of an
eskimo sold refrigerators iced tea at 2¢ a glass.
Want cheese? We're rats. Played no game playing
house all our lives. Settling: after 25 years
walked at night the streets of our marriage
to the forbidding old factory at the foot
of the unexpected turn into Gay Street our
Serpentine curve at the foot of that alley
with its brightly lit door lamps guarding nearly

200 year old two story village wooden houses
and Gay Street was almost gay but empty.

Cöthen .. the Schloss .. offered a more intimate setting
for the first *Brandenburg* .. conducted *in seinem Hause*
.. a 'Comödien-Theatrum' in the Orangery beyond the Schloss
.. little music .. Baldassare Galuppi but no Monteverdi, Corelli
.. the Prince owned a viola by Stainer dated 1650
.. Bach tuned the quill plectrums .. no one could
better to his satisfaction .. so skillful at it
took him no more than one quarter hour
.. 'tried to get a word in with Mr. Handel
for your (Bach's) sake .. could accomplish nothing, he
(Handel) a bit *touched* or so it seemed'
.. but not infrequent visitors .. occasions characters
                                    not stated ..
disturbed by the clatter of a water mill
beyond the Schloss Garden near the orangery .. walking
between sentries into the exercise ground .. sleek horses ..
'the window .. behind the organ .. should be built up
to shelter it from drafts .. ' would not compete
'had the angelic throng descended he'd have been rejected'
but did play for his old friend Reinken
.. extemporizing on "An Wasserflüssen Babylon" .. after which R
'I thought this art was dead, I see
it lives in you.' .. *À son altesse Marggraf
de Brandenbourg &c, &c* .. sometimes one purrs .. the
Six Brandenburg he probably never performed .. *Serenade Libretto*
for his Prince 'sight and seeing, breath and
singing' .. with him to Carlsbad .. shades of Saratoga ..
where the Prince took a bath? Then left for Leipzig
.. his son's first lesson in an exercise book
.. little clavier-book for Wilhelm Friedemann Bach first
started in Coethen 22 January 1720 (71 leaves).
Forgetting: that's all I need say or remember.

Midnight opening the door to the telephone ringing
(the violinist's timing always right) could not believe
the voice after two months' distance. 'P?' 'Yes
me.' 'What is't?' 'Naturally I phone because I've
something to ask.' What he *had*: our deep need.

An armory shattering, three levitating torahs flying thru
a Chagall see with her worries he with
his fiddle who with Whose bass *the trembling*
string the lighted ha' the red-head priest tempered
The Seasons Johann Sebastian his clavier, chances of
ordered changes changes of ordered chances, song that
literally came into and out of one's ears
seven horses run Pegasus flying to cleaning house
seven words heaven, eight love, nine universe, longing
that innocence at nine, a dip of the
valley shoots children skating red blue and snow:
writing '19 for 47 years later feeling that
moment that far back: millennia raiding to nations
and still their *yes* that means *no*. The
young said '*You old, to blame*—but we
who looked towards no nation, all regions peoples'?
That death should sing: the young live after.
Vietnamese story: Kung Buddha Christos and no forgiveness
not hard to die when gods likewise try?
'If it be now, 'tis not to come
if it be not to come, it will be now
if it be not now, yet it will come.'
'As dry pumps will not play till
water is thrown into them .. tho' I light
my Candle at my Neighbour's Fire does not
alter the Property, or make Wick Wax Flame
or the whole Candle less my own'—Swift

'of the great Scriblerus (works) made and to
be made, written and to be written, known
and unknown, this excellent person who may well
be called The Philosopher of Ultimate Causes
since by a Sagacity peculiar to himself
he hath discovered Effects in their very Cause
.. *A Demonstration of the Natural Dominion of the*
Inhabitants of the Earth over that of the
Moon .. *with the Proposal of a Partition-Treaty*
among the earthly Potentates: as to music Heidegger
has not the face to deny he has
been much beholden to his scores.'

Swift: 'As
I have a tender Regard to Men of
Great Merit, and Small Fortunes .. shall let slip
no Opportunity by bringing them to light, when
either through a peculiar Modesty or some .. Unhappiness ..
they have been unwilling to present themselves to
the World, and have been consequently no otherwise
remarkable in it, than by the Number
or Size of their Performances. This Piece of
Humanity was instilled into me by an accidental
Turn in my own Fortunes, which was owing
to the Discovery a Man of great Penetration
and Power made of the Excellence and Superiority
of my Genius.' The laughter without the mask:

'For poetry' (Scriblerus Aristotle) 'to be a success'
'as those in a Garden do from their own
Root and Stem .. I have observed a Gardener
cut the outward Rind of a Tree (which
is the Surtout of it) to make it
bear well .. why Wits of all Men living
ought to be ill clad.' (The grapevine heard:
'Have fun Henry R.') Then the old sang
the young as an other Swan read and considered
'we expect from others not to our latent powers
but to the position which we have attained.'
Then my constancy shyness said: 'The buoy exclaimed'
(not the sailor). That was no misprint nor
inept wit with her.

19

An other
   song—you
want another
   encóre I

hear back-
   stage the
stagehand's *late*
   the stage's

moon his
   sufferance of
lights   footcandles
   mind pines

at a
   door snow
flakes drift
   down up

thru and
   past turn
over under
   on froth

pine needles
   frost tomorrow's
sun better
   than any

tune   bōwed
   fingered drawn

lights dimmed
　　bōwed heart

another
　　bŏwed—fame
crowds an
　　other valentine.

No ill-luck
if bonding
tohu bohu
horsehair mends
azure　mane
flogs cold
races rut
shards the
perverse desŏlate
with pride
who curse
misfortune　Place
it futile range

less discreet
than her
lips dawned
on china
benign day's
first kiss
the lips
not drinking
yet where
to tarry
is breath:
arm even
the martyr's assay

will may
may be
soul owned
by time

illumine itself
primordial elect
penchant salute
horsehair silk
play to
the balm
of time
an anti-matter
of its sigh

bird one
hears once
of all
alive   comber
naked jubilation
its story
cinder sparing
the fire
fierce shying
idleness offense:
purchase   woman
child broth
quarryman cut out

for his
marriage   cobbler
who'd recreate
shoes (feet
if *you*
will revive
everyday's amities
his live
eye separate
him from
his togs
so he
walk naked god

song of
his wood

the truth
of a
face   of
it hymn
work patience
atlas herb
science ritual
while insensible
authority trouble
to humiliate
ore and motility

their impalpable
conscionable double
when no
eye'll hallucinate
air with
divisions   sage
sprig the
litigious who
tease but
till the
blossom grow
too large
for their reasons

fierce shyness
no symbol
literally Don
Quixote with
shoe trees
come home:
(Two lives
unknown to
each other
profess with
and without
salon a
future apart the

like hazard
sang wife
sang child)
Asked him
4-year old
'why the
violin?' responded
"Individually I
love it"
Finally—"you
don't understand
you're like
a sleeping frog."

PAGANINI PRIZE
.. Rules .. Violinists
of any
nationality, which
have not
overcome the
age of
35 .. can
compete .. required
a certificate
of birth
or the
like .. with eventual

papers relating
to musical
studies .. ad
every other
document .. the
competitor esteems
to produce ..
personal identification
when attending ..
FIRST TEST
Porpora (Carisch)

159

Bach *Ciaconna*
Paganini *Capriccio n. 23*

SECOND TEST
Mozart .. Paganini
two "Capricci"
(excluded the
one n.
23) Prokofieff
Scherzo THIRD
Concerto or
important composition
for violin
from Beethoven
up to
the modern Composers

(The Sonatas
for violin
and piano
are excluded)
PAGANINI *Concerto*
in D
Major first
tempo, with
cadence as
chosen by
the competitors
.. with orchestra
.. The competition will

take place
in Geneo
the selection
.. made privately
JURY The
Jury with
the Tecnical
Manager of
the Competition

as Chairman
will be
composed by
foreign and Italian

music-masters, whose
names will
be made
known, at
least three
months before
the expiration
termes fixed
for the
production of
applications .. the
choice of
the six (max)

competitors admitted
to the
final test
and the
final classification
based on
the whole
tests performance
will be
stated by
the Jury
whose judgement
will be inappelable

and issued
by majority
of manifest
votes. Considering
that the
1.st prize
is indivisible

the Jury
will be
at liberty
in case
classification should
be exceptionally difficult

to request
all or
part of
the finalists
to perform
other compositions
.. candidates having
successfully passed
selection will
be offered
a sejourn
in hotels
or boarding houses

.. for under
age competitors
signature of
father or
mother or
somebody their
substitute is
wanted .. must
reach Segretary's
office. The
winner will
play the
Paganini's violin at

Palazzo Tursi
on October
12 in
the evening
on occasion

162

of the
conclusive Ceremonies
of Columbus'
celebration and
will be
invited to
perform a
concerto during the

symphonic season
at the
Teatro Comunale
dell' Opera.
1.st PRIZE
Lit. 2.000.000
4.th   200.000
love's labour's lost
we (?) four
indeed confronted
four / In
Russian habit
a bullish violin

market with
bearish virtuosi
tuning nearly
anachronous the
public guts:
spit in
the hole,
man, and
tune again
considering 4.th
a bit
of luck
called forth the

honor of
1.st Prize
warm by

4's Mozart
an honest
Russian wish
that the
award had
gone the
other way
and not
the ways
of a *concours*

too the
Italian Chairman
uncomposed *segretly*
let 4.th
play *the*
Paganini's violin
two mornings
before official
Columbus night
a heavy
fiddle almost
the size
of a viola

good only
for pouncing
Paganini, scratchy
like stoked
cinders for
any Bach:
The roof
had rained
on Paganini
painted long
night before
wet the
serious lips smeared

smiled down
perhaps with

Whitman on
Jenny Lind
for "all
her blandishments
never touched
my heart
.. dexterity .. all
very pretty
.. leaps .. double
somersaults" their
time gone by

preempted by
the symphony's
summer festivals
week ends
displacing the
year round
tanglewoods and
small town
thugs by
inundations by
thousands music's
fools good
for their money

TV Day
Nippon a
thousand under
teens scratching
"Rondeau" together
(passing a
Funeral Parlor
'where people
are born
in this
town') all
contests decided
before the outcome

by the
Pythagoreans' Four
justice the
first perfect
square product
of equals
holy holy
tetraktys root
and source
generate gods
and men
(bless us)
divine number begins

with one
until it
comes to
Four then
it begets
can: must
placed: lifts
'See what
you thought
Four really
ten a
central fire
Triangle of Four

boundless breath
dying undying
the worded
reasons: The
Golden Words
and you
shall know
nature is
one and
neither hope
beyond hope

nor fail
of any truth.'

The wistaria   's
blessing: why
you should
have patience
ranging random
numbers (my
luck is
13) and
if I
voice thru
Demetrius 'Egypt
. . singing harmonies
of seven vowels

hymning gods'
(before phoneme)
' . . sequence men
listened to
. . voices replacing
flute and
lyre   diphthong
clashing diphthong
. . variety . . elevation
. . rough . . smooth
hoiain not
only different
letters   different breathings

concurrence of
like vowes
a bit
of song
trills   song
piled (so
to say)
on songs . . '
reminding me

167

'Die Elenden
sollen essen'
Bach's first
music (Leipzig Cantorate)

Phoenix   Paganini's
spidery legs
flying two
broken strings
hanging all
on one
string, patience
fire your
father's slaked
burning   I
had no
patience with
another who forecast

me hungry
then as
he had
been   drudging
professing to
make pure
the speech
of a
scrawling race
Sun no
hay State
exchanges' rolling
moss *mention distinguée*

son with
concert shoes
practical enough
poetic justice
that you
bring me
Le Livre

de Mallarmé
professor by
subsistence hazard
home where
else had
he to venture

shy and
or fierce
both our
chances staked
from the
same root
what notes
preyed playing
on us
a stretto
two dollar
orange tree
our living room

our lives
room   Pegasus
from Medusa
tho his
century's dice
resigned to
her forecasting
mine—engulfed
making all
of the
universe purely
of speech
I'd rather not

preempt my
horse from
actual pavement
or green
that's city

that's country
the rest
black or
white day
of a
last rare
mind cornered
by political beasts

But how
beautifully   a
last   mind
dies: 'What book?
what book?
entire enough
perfect enough
to take
the place
of all
the books
and of
the world itself

.. Piece or
that play
with concert
dialog poem
.. symphony for
scene .. bottom
de l'OE—'
towards (?) '(*vers*)
published one
time for
all .. under
one's HAT
all rendered virginal'

Foregone sublimations
of *Eureka*
'each fractioning

fragment the
ensemble's rhythm'
foreseeing *Wherever*
we put
our hats
is our
home: those
who do
not understand
may hurt and

those who
understand may
hurt as
Blaise Pascal's
candle pleaded
'no one
is offended
at not
seeing everything'
and the
Leonov first
to float
in space knows

he would
not meet
anyone there:
'The loan
from above
in favor
of all
the world
restored to
the people'
(*when* had
all?) Grape
arbor of little

Doric columns
sowing of

flourishes, arabesque
each conceivably
offend: 'Man
does not
write with
light on
black crystal
night .. in
black ink's
audacity .. married
to his night.'

Is the
man ink
and does
his 'white
paper support'
eyes the
fine day
he'll look
away from
black letters
to regret
sun (window)
is not theirs

If the
'crowd buy'
of the
inkwell what
'proof' one
ear's 'reciprocal'?
Pascal: paschal
'The last
thing settled
writing a
book .. what
one should
put in first'

And any
play performed
the 20th
anniversary of
Hiroshima's "A"
may as
well as
not have
 retched the
pinnacle, pitiful
the world's
lonely who
would love all

How generously
Mallarmé's late
thought minds
'the book
however seeming
never begins
or ends
.. the crowd
other than
by silence
takes part
exults as
choir .. voices .. vaults'

proposing 'the
State raise
a trifling
tax on
works in
the public
domain to
feed young
artists, the
classics' ideal
legatees (justice)

the only
imminent blue bloods'

Son and
young friends
for what
my work
is worth
let the
State pick
up his
suggestion for
you I
do not
need the
trifle nor'd live

it all
over again
for the
fee   my
test love
of the
drudgery involved
her quilt
and this
maybe not
too late
tribute to
once Stéphane Mallarmé

whose *Book*
prophesy say
his branch
brings to
our family.
The physician
Sextus Empiricus
anxious to
divorce metaphysics

174

from medicine
said that
'the art
of letters by

comprehension cures
a most
inactive disease
. . forgetfulness . . and
therefore has
its use
which the
conceited needlessly
inquisitive enfeeble'
Against the
Professors showed
'the subject
taught does not

exist, nor
the teacher
nor the
learner nor
the method
. . the óbverse
perceptible by
all alike
. . speech by
agreement plain
to those
who apprehend
its objects . . reviving

what is
known'   not
for the
footling question
But for
the eye
that appears

larger seeing
nine tenths
of ills
from stubborn
intelligence   Unknown
friends are few

no friends
unless intimately
accessible   Intellect
resigned to
less is
susceptible at
least to
the range
of two
sides of
a coin
Some   few
see its edge

so increscent
to possibilities
flipping a
coin may
decide, the
sufferance of
intellect is
the body's
plight for
at least
two   true
Sextus need
not offend Pythagoras

calling his
'wrong moment
foolish for
sobering frenzied
youths with

a righteous
spondean' (instead
of quitting
their dive)
Aseptic doctor
practice the
cure for
forgetfulness   sometimes no

way *out*
Either way
too easy
for tutor
to be
his own
tooter   Lunik's
hunch moon
surface desolate
porous rock:
Dogs permitted
only in
Elevator No. 3

Alighieri threading
a needle
a millennium
after Gai's
spindle: the
astronauts' violent
spinning docking
"God? we
were busy"
(West of
Vatican Belvedere
Apollo "By
God a Mohawk")

Chatillon 'fevered
with ivy
poison .. solaced

with tobacco
and Shakespeare'
burn to
ascend. On
the day
when the
elephant of
the map
India draw
the yellow pincers

of China
or our
air cavalry
go into
the sea
Japan gravel
temple gates
broken lopped
branches stumped
trunks of
trees tapestries
hang reverse
sides   the new

time of
forgetting pier
and lintel
for advantage
of being
slid thru
a door
lying down
all appointments
of elimination
on one
no standing
dire past to

sit down:
the quicker

to get
with computers
to Invisible
Media from
the old
arts' fetters
(the aged
Cardinal wishes
his fish
peddler's voice
not to disturb

Mozart's *Requiem*
sung for
the late
President, enlightened
His Holiness
that His
medical advice
is not
privileged with
Infallibility or
it would
be fatal
for ulcers

while the
Viennese director
of opera
still thinks
Sacco/Vanzetti
are a
pair of
lovers   the
old singer
a bit
of a
schlemiel sips
the young's gift

'nectar of
heather-honey gathering
of herbs
under the
full moon
.. a formula
fiercely battled
over guarded
by Eire's
ancient warriors'
drop of
Irish Mist
with its red

ribboned tag
of blarney
reading it
drowses knows
like the
diver could
it walk
under water
it would
have walked
here from
Ireland   splayfoot
snow on pineneedles

night snow
sounds rain
thru trees
morning snow
ploughs will
not hurry
a path
A legacy
windfall of
a rush
of notes

falling together
album celestial valentine

Mallarmé (not
the hat)
the face
a covert
look might
make one
shy of
song   *From*
thence sorrow
be *ever*
raʒ'd   nine
so soon twenty

20

Respond for P.Z.'s tone row
At twenty

Variants

An

Octet [Orders]
13 Pomes, A Prelude & A Postlude
Ecce Puer
The title …
Combination Block
for a dancer
3 pieces for unaccompanied clarinets

groupings and quartet for Saxophone,
Trumpet, Mandolin, & Double Bass
Piano pieces nos. 1 & 2
Piano piece no. 3
Percussion

Ecce puer
for a dancer
Piano piece no. 3
Piano pieces nos. 1 and 2
Variants
13 Pomes, A prelude and A postlude
Combination block
groupings and quartet for Saxophone,
Trumpet, Mandolin & Double Bass
Octet [Orders]
Percussion
3 pieces for unaccompanied clarinets
The title …

13 Pomes, A Prelude & A Postlude
Ecce Puer
Variants
groupings and quartet for Saxophone,
   Trumpet, Mandolin & Double Bass
Octet [Orders]
The title of this piece is
  the title of this piece doesn't matter
Percussion
3 pieces for unaccompanied clarinets
Combination block
Piano pieces nos. 1 & 2
Piano piece no. 3
for a dancer

Variants
13 Pomes, A prelude and A postlude
3 pieces for unaccompanied clarinets
for a dancer
groupings and quartet for Saxophone,
   Trumpet, Mandolin & Double Bass
Octet [Orders]
The title ...
Percussion
Combination block
Piano pieces nos. 1 and 2
Piano piece no. 3
Ecce puer

nine

oh ivy green

oh ivy green, so soft and green
thou that do cover the earth and wall,
I pray to know what makes me worship thee,
Thou that do cover do make travelers stand
While Robins do nest in thy leaves
While crickets do hum their song
and bees do fly around thee
What is it, I wonder that makes thee
     so loved

183

21

RUDENS

dedicated to
the memory of John Gassner and
my brother Morris Ephraim

21

RUDENS

PROLOGUE

(*Voice off*)

> an 'twere any nightingale
> an if they be not
>   sprites

Plot

fisheRman's sea   net dragged Up a leathery wicker
rattling the baby's charms of his master's Daughter
a leno had kidnapped for his slave brothEl.
unknown to her father she was his little ward
after her shipwreck: later they fouNd out—
she married her Sweetheart   a young man.
(*Voice off continues to read across and down*)

PERSONAE	CHARACTERS
ARCTURUS PROLOGUS	ARCTURUS
SCEPARNIO SERVUS	SCAPE hired to DADS
PLESIDIPPUS ADULESCENS	PLACEY a young man
DAEMONES SENEX	DADS an old man
PALAESTRA ⎱ PUELLAE	POLLY ⎱ girls
AMPELISCA ⎰	AMABEL ⎰ hired to LENO
PTOLEMOCRATIA SACERDOS VENERIS	OLD DOLLY sacred to Venus
PISCATORES	FISHERMEN
TRACHALIO SERVUS	TRACK hired to PLACEY
LABRAX LENO	LENO or PIMP
CHARMIDES SENEX	CHUM old friend of LENO
LORARII	2 WHIPS
GRIPUS PISCATOR	GREAVE fishes for DADS

187

Who moves men maritime landlubbers
I'm of His Celestial City.
See *here* splendent stellar candid
sign forever timely the season's
earth sky name's Arcturus: me.
Nightly clear sky with Gods
with strollers amble secretly days.
Falling stars are no accident:
Gods' umpire and men's, Jupiter
He knows gents' starry paths
factoring human mores piety faith
making us judges of opulence.
Who's false in's little testimonials
petty kickback inured abjured impecunious
our scrip refers to Jove
quotidian Seer wary of malice.
Whose littlest hopes postulate perjury
malice's wraths falsehoods impetrating justice
such judgment Jove again judges
mulcts multifold their legal parings.
Blest men earn other scrip.
Curs mull thick to assume
Jove'll be plastered by donations:
operatic scenes whiff ordure to
Him whose need's past soliciting.
Face it *pious* simply earns
has more grace than venom.
I take it you're good
quick to life piously faithful:
retain its pores facts enlighten.
Enough eloquence, my plot's rather—

primum mobile—Plautus' Diphilus called
that town Cyrene. Look, Dads'
farmhouse is by the sea.
Old Athenian homeless, how, malice?
ever a patriot left her
Athens: stuck with her mud,

cheated of everything, dealing kindly,
his little baby daughter robbed
by raider for worst trader—
our Leno's virgin of Cyrene.
A friendly Attic youngster's seen
her with her lyre from school:
she has him occupied, off
to Leno to buy her,
paying down, contracting the balance.
This Leno custom made fickle
reneged on the youngster's bargain.
His partner an old Sicilian
sellout from Agrigentum visiting him
(alluding to the virgin's form
and the other miraculous girls)
urged they go pronto to
Sicily together "where the voluptuaries
ride gaily we'll lasso dividends."
Persuaded. Leno stowed ship last
night absconded with his goodies
after he'd told his adolescent
client Leno had to pray
to Venus, whose Fane's—*right*—
behind me, but after that
to come here for lunch.
Leno sailed with his girls
the youngster heard the story
and has run to the
port where the ship disappeared.

I saw her wronged, supported
the virgin, I rattled Leno
in creepy hibernal flood tides.
I'm Arcturus, star most acerb,
vehemence rising down more vehement.

Now both shipwrecked Leno and
Chum sit on a rock.
Virgin and another lovable, too
safe jumping ship to skiff

swirl past rock to land—
old Dads' home in exile,
wind dislodged roof's falling shingles.
That's his servant carrying the
spade. The adolescent coming, the
boy who bought from Leno.
We're all soldiers, take care!

ACT I 1

> *ye lightnings, ye thunders—*

Scape

Prodigal immortals what a tempest
Neptune blew off last night
belching our roof up—wind?
I'll say wind, Euripides' *Alcmena*
mess of stucco and shingles
with glorious light and windows.

I 2

Placey, 3 Dumbshow Officers, Scape, Dads

PL.   I've wasted your good time
rushing you here for nothing
not catching Leno in port.
Hope's never idle, friends—why!
my persistence repressed your duties,
run back!—How's Venus, *fain*
where he'd sacrifice my lunch?
SC.   Scape sap! better mix loam!
PL.   Who spoke now?
DA.   Hey, Scape!
SC.   Who's whining?
DA.   Remember I paid.
SC.   That's calling me swine, Dads.
DA.   Use this mud, dig man.
My villa needs a whole
roof to seal *this* hole.
PL.   Salvé daddy—'lo too.
DA.   Salutations.
SC.   Who're you, boy or girl
'dad-dée'?
PL.   He-man.
SC.   Bore your own.

DA.   I had a daughter. Lost.
No sons.
PL.   God may yet—
SC.   Give *you* Hercules' club for
piddling here while *we're* working.
PL.   Your house, daddy?
SC.   What's your
game, investigating to rob later?
PL.   This louse must be groomed
for probate, daddy, you permit
him to attack his superior?
SC.   Poor scum and impudence to
take on and molest us
like debtors.
DA.   Take care, Scape—
What's up, lad?
PL.   Unfortunately this
lout eructed to interrupt you,
but may I ask without
offense—
DA.   Spill tho I'm working.
SC.   Why don't you pollute th'bog,
cut thatch—nice wether—
DA.   Quiet!
—Talk free, son.
PL.   Please, have
you seen a curly grayhaired
malicious perjurer and flatterer—
DA.   Many.
Enough to make life miserable.
PL.   Particularly a man with two
girls in Venus' temple, prinked
for sacrifice yesterday or today?
DA.   No luck, son, haven't come
across any sacrifices lately: worshippers
never could escape me—borrowing
my water, kindling, saucepan, knife,
spit, tripe-tripod—what have you?
Venus who owns my kitchen
and well recently spares me.

PL. I hear you and perish.
DA. Lad I'm all for you.
SC. Hey you starveling of Venus
better go home for lunch!
DA. So? a friend invited you
and hasn't shown up?
PL.   Yes.
SC. No chance you'll lunch here:
you should date Ceres the
caterer—Venus hungers for love.
PL. The lewdness of it burns.
DA. Prodigal immortals! look seawards, Scape—
men or washouts?
SC.   Looks like
these burnt out before lunch.
DA. How?
SC.   Bathing after yesterday's dinner.
DA. Here's their ship, wrecked.
SC.   Like
your landed villa, shingle.
DA.   Whew!
How, little men, réjects swimming?
PL. Where are these men?
DA.   Right—
see—down shore—
PL.   I see
maybe that scum! we're off!
take care!
SC.   Don't remind *me*.
By Palaemon Neptune's saintly comrade
Hercules' sockdologer like seadogs crow
what a view!
DA.   View?
SC.   Miraculous!
two girls in one skiff!
Affliction, misery! Good! Good! Splendid!
Skiff clears the shore's rocks,
no steersman could steer better!
Never seen such seas! Safe
if they escape the undertow!

Now now's perilous! Under! into—
the shallows! Swims! *Cutie Pie!*
Rises, walks this way! Praises!
Her timid friend abandoned the
skiff, struck her knees hitting
the water. Safe too, yet
reeling right she goes wrong
on my blessed day.
DA.　　　　　Concerned?
SC.　If the rock breaks her
back what's to depend on?
DA.　If you dream vesper snacks
with them join them, Scape,
if at home serve me.
SC.　Equity rules.
DA.　　　　　After me.
SC.　　　　　　　　　Sir!

I 3

(*Voice off*)
　　　nine
　　　men's
　　　morris

　　　this
　　　is
　　　my
　　　form

　　　a
　　　voice
　　　blown

Palaestra

Polly

Man's misery suffers less remembered,
his story dissolves his bitterness.
Is God pleased I'm stripped
fearfully in this strange country?

194

Can anyone born remember this,
call this *paid* for piety?
I couldn't labor a point
against parent or god—impiety!
sad paragon virtuous as I
was—indecórous, iniquitous, immodest—
who, gods? How will you
try evil, by dishonoring innocence?
Now if I knew myself
or parents feckless I'd not
pity us. Leno's scurrility festers:
his ship and cargo foundered
I'm all the relics left.
She drowned—no skiff: alone.
Dear friend, if she were
safe she'd lighten my despair.
No one consoles me, I'm
alone one with this place,
here rock here sea groans
no man comes my way:
these rags endow my dowry,
no sop or sleep welcomes,
hope's mist, must I live?
I will never know here.
Show me the way out
someone, show me a narrow
path—here or there riddles,
nothing here grows I see.
Cold, loss, fear tear me
and my parents don't know
my misery, torn from them
born free presumably to quicken
sorrow, judged like the poor,
little profit life brought them.

I 4

Amabel, Polly

AM.   Corporeal death's best secluded, my
heart melts in animal throes.

spare hopes don't delight me
scurrying after my lost companion
with voice, eyes and ears,
nor can I think running
everywhere where to find her—
cruel stones, if she lives
I'll live so she'll live.
PO.   Whose voice sounds so near?
AM.   Pity me—whose? here?
PO.   Benign hope seek and save
me, exhume me from misery!
AM.   The voice of a girl!
PO.   A girl's! I heard it.
Amabel, you?
AM.   My Polly, you?
PO.   I must call out louder—
Amabel!
AM.   My! who?
PO.   I, Polly!
AM.   Say where!
PO.   Really in trouble.
AM.   So'm I! We're a pair.
I'm dying to see—
PO.   Lovely—
AM.   Our voices are game! Where!
PO.   Echo me! Come! *here*.
AM.   Hold
PO.   —my hand.
AM.   Here!
PO.   Dear, say *alive*.
AM.   You wish me alive again
touching you. I cannot believe
my arms embrace, close dear
promise, my troubles leave me.
PO.   You speak from *my* lips,
we'd better go—
AM.   how, love?
PO.   By the shore.
AM.   Sure, love,
sopping wet as we are?

196

PO.   Whatever comes need is perpetual—
look there!
AM.   Where?
PO.   See a—
fane!
AM.   Where?
PO.   To our right.
AM.   Dressed for the gods indeed!
PO.   Pretty! so men are near.
Dear God who rules here
save! judge our deep need.

I 5

(*Voice off*)
                pomegranate open our song
                And what an if
                his sorrows have so
                overwhelm'd   and the worst
                fall that ever fell
                'to know everything
                is to die'
                the matter decided find
                the decision not ours
                to mull 'it cannot
                hurt purity to love
                .. all great amusements are
                dangerous .. none more to
                be feared than .. our
                play .. by which the
                fear of pure souls
                is removed'   love values
                does not compete   push
                the cat *posses*   some
                time   the art rots
                beautifully   '*A made a*
                finer end   'A parted
                and smile upon his
                fingers' ends

OL.   Who invokes my patroness's mercy?
Voices prayers call me forth.
My goddess is benevolent, not
grudging, seek her she's forgiving.
PO.   Good day, mother.
OL.   Blessings girls,
from where under heaven do
you come in these rags?
PO.   By chance just now alongshore
but long before from afar.
OL.   On the seas' blue, wood
horse's wake?
PO.   Admittedly.
OL.   Better white
garments carried offerings, the Fane's
holy, soiled attire is immodest.
PO.   How can two wrecks from
the sea bring you offerings?
We beg at your knees
in want knowing no hope:
receive us under your roof
embrace our misery pity it—
we are lost expecting nothing—
in rags as you see.
OL.   Hands my dears! get up!
Misery makes me no less
a woman poor as you
life is bare serving Venus.
AM.   Heavens is this Venus Fane?
OL.   Fact and in holiness I
serve love. Welcome to what
little's here while it avails.
Come in.
PO.   You honor us
mother.
OL.   But with my heart.

(*Voice off*)
>pomegranate
>chewed
>and
>spit
>spittle
>drowning
>worlds

Fishermen

Eking a pauper's living's misery
unskilled in finance or technique:
Necessity's cud and that's that.
Our decorations reveal we're plutocrats:
fishhooks, fishing-rods—profit and culture
daily maritime prodding for pabulum
exercise—gymnastics and wrestling bouts.
Urchins, lickrocks, oysters, acornshells, purplefish,
seanettles, mussels, lampshells: we trawl;
off the rocks fish aggressively.
Our capture's seafood. Eventually
no haul: salt bathed pure
we clink home, sleep supperless.
While the flood heaves us
hopelessly it's clams or perfection.
Pray Venus for grace today.

(*Voice off*)
>*as first the*
>*Lark when she*
>*means to rejoice*
>
>*the Nightingale another*
>*of my airy*
>*creatures that at*

midnight the earth
feeds—and carries
horses that carry

us   Not dull

II 2

Track, Fishermen

TR.   I've looked since employer Placey
bound first for port arranged
we'd meet at Venus Fane.
Who're those stars—standbys? boy!
Salvé! maritime furies, Conch Hookandeye's!
famished family, how goes? dying?
FI.   As usual, fishy: hungry, thirsty.
TR.   Law'nd disorder have you seen
a flushed strenuous young face
with three cloaked dummy machétes?
FI.   We've seen no such faces.
TR.   Nor warmed to potbellied Silenus
old braided eyebrows fraudulent forehead
stinking before gods and men—
leading two miracles to Venus?
FI.   Such distinguished native virtue should
come by hanging not Venus.
TR.   I *just* asked did you
see him.
FI.   No, luckily—goodbye!
TR.   Goodbye! *Damn* as I suspected
Leno stood up Placey, hauled
our girls away: I foretold
the pimp's lunch—sclerósed semen.
Well I'll mellow till my
peer comes, if I see
Old Dolly check with her.

(*Voice off*)
            fane

Amabel, Track

AM.   I follow: 'ask at this
villa nextdoor Venus for water'
TR.   Loveliness voiced!
AM.   Gracious who! Do
I see?
TR.   Isn't't Amabel—fain?
AM.   *Isn't* it Track, Placey's follower?
TR.   'Tis!
AM.   Track, hullo!
TR.   Hullo Amabel!
howdy—
AM.   Aged into malice.
TR.   No!
AM.   Sensible people fable the truth.
Where's Placey, playboy?
TR.   Now really!
inside, where else?
AM.   Not true.
TR.   No?
AM.   That's true.
TR.   Not me Amabel
but when's lunch?
AM.   Lunch, sweetness?
TR.   Nymphs holy offerings.
AM.   Asleep, sugar?
TR.   Honest—your employer Leno invited
mine to lunch.
AM.   Wonderful mistake!
gods' cheat Leno fakes again.
TR.   Neither of you sacrificing?
AM.   Silly—
TR.   What *are* you here for?
AM.   Safe from trouble poor orphans,
Old Dolly shelters Polly and me.
TR.   Polly, Placey's girl, *here?*
AM.   Safely!

TR.   Such lovely confidence my Amabel—
but what about those troubles?
AM.   Wrecked, Track, shipwrecked last night.
TR.   Ship—wrecked? Fabling?
AM.   Hasn't my
nitwit heard Leno clandestinely packed
us for Sicily with all
he owned? All now sunk.
TR.   *Neptune wise with your dice,*
perfect crapshooter lulled perjury low—
Where's Leno now?
AM.   *Perished drinking*
Neptune's full schooners—I 'pine—
TR.   *Downed* last night's lees—love
you, Amabel, sweet punning thing!
who saved you and Polly?
AM.   Stop squeezing, foxy! horrified we
jumped, our ship foundering towards
the rocks, into its skiff:
loosed its hawser—freed by
the tempest from the crew,
whaled by wind thru night
which exhumed us this dawn.
TR.   *Headsman Neptune scuttles the trash.*
AM.   Watch *your* head!
TR.   *Yours* dear!
I suspected Leno would. *I*
should grow hair, cast horoscopes.
AM.   You and your friend's forecasts!
TR.   What could *he* do?
AM.   Do?
Watched her night and day.
Placey's castoff probes his love.
TR.   Why Amabel!
AM.   Don't palm me!
TR.   Skin too? It's as with
bathers and clothesstealers hard to
catch: the clothes are stolen.
Thief sees victim, victim misses.
Take me inside.

AM.   Go yourself
where she weeps to Venus.
TR.   Weeps? It hurts—
AM.   tortured. Leno's
wreck buries her jewelbox baby
charms which reveal her parentage.
TR.   Where was it?
AM.   In Leno's
wicker—stolen to defame her.
TR.   Fox! so he'd sell her!
AM.   Think! all's there under water
with Leno's gold and silver.
TR.   Maybe charms don't capsize.
AM.   Sad
she's uncertain.
TR.   I'll go and
console her: it happens, *luck
comes to the hopeless unexpected.*
AM.   Another moral, *hope deceives some.*
TR.   I'll take, *self-hardened mollifies*—going
in unless you need me.
AM.   Yes, go—I'll obey Old—
Dolly, and ask for water nextdoor:
say *for Dolly* she said.
I've never seen a lady
worth more to gods and
men. Readily she bathed jetsam
like little things just born,
hitched her gown, warmed water:
there wasn't enough, I must
hurry and knock. Anybody in?

II 4

Scape, Amabel

SC.   Crackbrain! who's forcing our door?
AM.   I'm—
SC.   Hem! edible little woman!

AM. Hello—gentleman.
SC.   Hullo, little girl!
AM. Could you—
SC.   Come tonight yes
when I can, I work mornings
lovely thing—
AM.   Not so familiarly
please hands off—
SC.   Prodigal immortals, Venus
her eyes! What a body!
Owl bright—a wild brunette
what skin, breasts and lips!
AM. I'm not like that, don't
maul me—
SC.   This little bit?
AM. Later leisurely, now my errand
presses, please—yes or no?
SC. What's your wish?
AM.   The pitcher
pleads.
SC. And don't I plead?
AM. Old Dolly needs water *now*.
SC. I'm dispenser, not one drop—
I shafted this well—not
a drop unless you're sweet.
AM. Anybody is generous with water.
SC. *Somebody* is generous with more.
AM. O but I am, lover—
SC. Cutie Pie! calling me lover!
The water's yours for love,
I'll take your pitcher!
AM.   Here
hurry, fare—
SC.   one second, love!—
AM. What shall I tell Old Dolly—
I dilly-dallied? Sea's still stormy.
Heavens! the dead're down shore!
Mister Leno and his Sicilian
neither perished after all, always
more trouble than we rated.

I must run and warn
Polly, we'll be safer at
the altar until Leno presses
us, better not wait here.

II 5

Scape

Prodigal immortals, I believe water
is voluptuous. Love's traction hauled:
deep was the well speeding
my work. Pride don't sin—
but love is cocky today!
Here's your water, little belle.
Carry it honest like me.
Delectable—water—Where are you!
My she loves me! Hiding,
love? Taking your pitcherful? Where—
you're not timid—are you? Gentility?
Hercules leaves me. Deluded me.
Dumb pitcher set for th'ground,
what if someone stole you
sacred urn of Venus? My
fault! Insidious mule planned trapping
me with Venus's sacred urn—
fair play for the clink,
the magistrate and a lynching!
The mark on the pitcher
sings who owns it. Holy
Venus I'm for her door!
Hi! Old Dolly take your
pitcher, a little girl littered
here—must *I* carry it?

II 6

(*Voice off*)

> nothing to be got now-adayes
> unless thou canst fish—
> Op-and-Pop art, bare engineers bare

'what the traffic will bear'
a playes and tumbles, great
ones eat up little ones:
that *gives heauen countlesse*
eyes to view mens actes.
Think, in the height of
this bath, cool'd glowing hot
in that surge a horse-shoe
hissing hot—throng'd up with
cold . . chill: buy and die.
Honestly rich or contentedly poor
if a man can't curse his
friend whom *can* he curse?

Leno, Chum

LE.   Man's wilfully miserable mendicant crediting
Neptune his body and soul.
The sea spills its mix
racks him home "yours truly."
Polled Liberty is neat spurning
membership in Hercules' Seaman's Club.
Where's my chum o Perdition?
Ah he's coming!
CH.   Gripes! Leno
it's hard chasing strenuous equity!
LE.   You thing for eyes' sties
would you'd been crucified in
Sicily before all this misery.
CH.   You're one! if only I'd
sense to sleep over in
jail that day, Gods! may
your life's guests be you!
LE.   Misfortune was what I invited
sclerosis listened to your auscultations.
What incensed me to sail
and bury all I had?
CH.   Pole! minimal mirror! the ship
fractured from your ill-begot goods.
LE.   Pest your coaxing did it.

206

CH. Those sclerosed snacks you served
worse than Thyestes' or Tereus'.
LE. Hold my head, I'm sick.
CH. Puling lungs vomit you vomit.
LE. Polly, Amabel where are you!
CH. Feeding the fishes pabulum: *credo*!
LE. Your mendacious tool of tongue
magnified auscultation worked my mendicity.
CH. Boneache, be grateful, my work
salted the herring you were.
LE. Go to—stop crucifying me!
CH. Ye-es. I'm just as accommodating.
LE. You can't live my misery.
CH. I'm ever more miserable, Leno.
LE. Come?
CH.   You're deserving, I'm not.
LE. O lucky fortunate driedout thatch
bulrush serving glory in aridity!
CH. Me, I'm for light exercise
all my coruscations fable trembling.
LE. Eddy-polled Neptune you frigid bathman
my investments are soaked icecold!
CH. No thermopile yet instructs his
pouring potions of freezing salt.
LE. Fortunate the forgers of iron
sitting by charcoal: ever cuddled!
CH. Fortunate is the duck's uterus,
comes out of water dry.
LE. I could play an ogre!
CH. Come?
LE.   Hear my teeth crackle?
CH. I deserve my lavatory.
LE.   Come?
CH. For sailing aboard your ship—
fundamentally you made those waves.
LE. You rascal you promised me
the maximum profit in prostitutes,
windfalls to accrue you said.
CH. You positively figured you bullock
you'd eat up Sicily whole.

LE. Wonder what bullock devoured my
wicker pack's gold and silver—
CH. Undoubtedly the breed that devoured
the moneypouch in my sack.
LE. I'm reduced to my underwear
and this motheaten pallium—ruins.
CH. We're the same illicit society,
equal and partners.
LE.   Salvation'd be
if my little miracle girls
were safe. That young scut
Placey's option on Polly will
yet make trouble for me.
CH. Stultified weeper with *that* polecat,
tongue wagging you'll be solvent!

(*Voice off*, antiphon: *Leno, Chum*)
    LE. Nip & Tuck   Jimtown   Rake Pocket
    CH. Hog Eye Steal Easy Possum Trot
    LE. Flat Heel   Shake Rag   Poverty Slant
    CH. Black Ankle   Short Pone   Pig Misery
    LE. Yaller Flower of the Forest
    CH. Drag out any man   Ten-strikers!
    LE. How's yo' horse, Tarheel?
Is he religious?
    CH. Moke!
    LE. Jimpescute.
    CH. Juicy-spicy.
    LE. Leonine!
    CH. Leno?
    LE. Something grasps even if lunatic.
    CH. Not too hard to distinguish
a friend from a Pinkerton.

II 7

Scape, Leno, Chum

SC. Nuts! two little girls inside
hugging Venus praying and sobbing

scared miserably whining the sea
capsized them both this morning.
LE.   Gracious! Youth, *where* are they?
SC.   Sacrarium.
LE.   How *many?*
SC.   Count: you, me.
LE.   Mine?
SC.   Dunno!
LE.   Good-looking?
SC.   I'll say
I'll take love either half-stewed.
LE.   Little girls?
SC.   Go look yourself.
LE.   My little girls, old Chum!
CH.   Jump in the lake, yes?
LE.   I'm for Venus *now*!
CH.   *Maledictions*—
Sir, any place to sleep?
SC.   Everywhere's free to the public.
CH.   See I'm dripping, lend me
some dry clothes while these
dry, as I'd for you?
SC.   My rush hat's dry—want't?
Covers *me* when it rains.
Let me strip you first.
CH.   Hey the storm cleaned me!
SC.   Clean or greased I trust
you like chewed pomegranate—security!
Drip, freeze, rot or fare well
I don't house foreigners, see!
CH.   Going then? gone. Venal duck!
has no heart. What's th'use.
Try Venus Fane, sleep't off—
had more seadrink than cheer.
Cheap Greek wines, Neptune pouring
in his saltwater for purgative.
What's the word? A little
sleep, purged forever. At least
alive: what's jolly Leno conniving—

Dads

Miraculously gods playfellows dream in
men, don't let us sleep:
like me last night dreaming
this weird and silly dream:
a swallow's nest, a monkey
climbing to molest could not
grip what was in it,
then came down to me
asked to borrow a ladder.
I responded "by their example
Philomela and Procne engendered swallows"—
pleading "don't hurt my populace."
And the monkey fired ferociously
threatening all kind of evil
invoking justice. Somehow angered I
gripped her middle and looped
the monkey with her tail.
How'm I to divine this
dream—I've conjectured all day.

(Voice off)
> *middle summer's spring* and regret
> will with passing regret less
> unaware of one's own passing
> look to tree from morris
> dust—

DA.   But what's happening in Venus
Fane—Clamors? Oratory? Miraculous world!

III 2

Track, Dads, Two Dumbshow Whips

TR.   Whoa Cyrene's populace Implore faithful
Ah gruelled cult Colléct neighbors

Fortify hope by punishing poisoners
Vindicate piety Let no impiety
overpower innocence that notoriety scarifies
Stall impudicity Dot purity's premium
Foster law Nor victim quiver!
Hurry to Venus Fane implored faithful
Hear Hear my clamor Now
Fortify suppliants of Venus institutes
Morals antique custom commiserate maidenhair
Collar sin's tool before't worms—
DA.   Why stuck, negotiant?
TR.   Senator, on
my knees, please—
DA.   Let go me!
What's this raving!
TR.   Narthex asafetida
syrups in futures the year's
safe shipments to Capua, listen—
no colds lipsore sore eyes—
DA.   Nuts?
TR.   May their seed multiply,
just listen help me, senator.
DA.   By your shins, ankles, posterior
itching for a year's harvest
vintage whipping with elm-rods I'll
teach your insolence to rave!
TR.   You curse—I blest you.
DA.   That was blessing, it's deserved.
TR.   I ask again—
DA.   What!
TR.   Two
innocent girls there need help—
worsted despite law and justice,
attacked right in Venus Fane,
old Sacred Lady is threatened!
DA.   What man's so confident dare
violate Sacred Lady, who *are*
the girls, what's *his* iniquity?

    'What altar 'll shelter a man
    outraging reason! What is denial
    if not reason rejecting assent?
    Nothing is said so rightly
    it cannot twist into wrong'

TR.   Listen! They embrace Venus a
curst sort tears them from.
They cry to be free.
DA. Who's so ungodly—speak, man!
TR.   A lecherous fraud, parricide, perjurer-plenipotentiary
lawcorrupt impure impudence voraciously nondescript
Leno! Who'll word his predicament!
DA. A pole his hanging predicament!
TR.   He'd choke holiness into lechery—
DA. Hercules! he'll pay for it!
Turbalio! Sparax! Hey Whips!
TR.   Help
them!
DA. No second imperatives!

    (Enter Whips)

                  Follow!
TR.   Glide his eyes cooked cuttlefish!
DA. Pig! Bounce the stuck sow!
TR.   How dear are the fistfalls
I hear his teeth falling—
See! hurrying my frightened girls!

(Voice off)
    Switch is a whip
    which never has been

III 3

Polly, Track, Amabel

PO. Now we've come to nothing
a silly uprising no tenet

no speculation solution for it
we've no way out anywhere:
both of us embarrassed together
his importunity mounted to injury
forcing himself on us there—
inside—scandalously assaulting Old Dolly
rumpling pulling her without qualm—
tearing us from Venus's image.
If Fortune must ravage us
Death's more suitable, better dead
than in misery.
TR.   What'n oration!
I'll console her. How's Polly!
PO.   Who spoke?
TR.   Amabel!
AM.   I'm scared!
who's't!
PO.   names me!
TR.   Expecting sees.
PO.   My hopeful!
TR.   Look to me!
PO.   Ward off his hands or
I'll die by my own.
TR.   Ah *that's* inept.
PO.   Don't joke,
Track, you must, he's serious.
AM.   Rather than Leno—maul me,
Death, yet my woman's mind
trembles thru me, bitter day!
TR. Animation, my babies!
PO.   Invent it?
TR.   Sit down by that altar!
AM.   Why's't more prodigious than Venus
inside we've been torn from?
TR.   Sit down! I'll guard you,
this altar your walled defense—
Venus Protectress—I'll encounter Leno!
PO. (& AM.)   We'll sit and, Alma Venus,
weeping embrace your altar, kneel
Nixi, praying Mother receive us.

213

Punish those who belittle your
Fane, shield us, its peace.
Neptune washed us up naked,
don't be angry, we're virgin
whatever bit unwashed we appear.
TR.   Venus, I believe they're intelligent!
Redeem innocent fears trembling! You
born from an oyster shouldn't
spurn pearls—old Dads comes!

(*Voice off cantabile*)
               Like a—
               mg. dancer
               carries what—
               sashay in—
               her hand—
               for an—
               Under Ground

               Toe Mickle
               could not
               do better'n
               blowing
               cold and
               hot

III 4

Dads, Polly, Amabel, Track, Leno, Whips

DA.   Out of the Fane, abomination!
You! sit there! Where're they?
TR.   Here!
DA.   Wonderful! he'll not dare!
Corrupt gods' law would you?
Punch his nose!
LE.   Remember, righteousness!
DA.   Audacious, man?
LE.   You're robbing my
girls—that's *rape*.

TR.   Let any
responsible senator of Cyrene decide
if they're yours or free,
if you should be incarcerated
for life, outfoot the clink.
LE.   Not your day gallows-bird—oldtimer
I'm calling *you.*
DA.   Dispute *him.*
LE.   No, *you!*
TR.   *Me! Your* girls?
LE.   You say.
TR.   Dare tag them!
LE.   Touch'n' go?
TR.   I'll hang you
for a punchingbag, beat Hell—
LE.   Can't take m'own from Venus?
DA.   No, our law won't allow—
LE.   I don't trade your laws.
I'll have my girls now,
oldtimer, or your cash: if
Venus pleasures let her pay.
DA.   Goddess render coin? Listen: dare
one lewd sally jokingly, I'll
drain tar out of you.
Whips, when I nod, blacken his
eyes! or my whip'll be
rush around myrtle!
LE.   That's *assault.*
TR.   You protést, rotter?
LE.   Bum! three-termer, *you* insult *me?*
TR.   Say I'm *that,* 'n' you're noble,
legally they're free girls.
LE.   Free?
TR.   Hercules yes! and Grecian girls:
this one of Athenian parentage.
DA.   What?
TR.   Born in Athens, free.
DA.   Of my people?
TR.   Aren't you
Cyrenaic?

DA.   No, Attic—born, bred—
TR.   God! Senator, defend two compatriots.

(*Voice off—Dads'*)
          I look on common sorrow—
          three then—grown her age—
          my daughter

LE.   I paid cash
for both to their owner—
Athenian or Theban they're servants.
TR.   Kidnapper Mouser of virgins, beast
grinding, exchanging them like counters!
The other whose pedigree I
don't know 's pure too—scum!
LE.   You're her standby.
TR.   Tripes, strip!
If your back hasn't more
stripes than nails'n a fo'c's'le
I'm top liar. *After you—*
inspect mine: if it isn't
guarantee tight leather wine-flask, absolutely
all of one piece, why
shouldn't I whip you sick?
Still peeking at them? I'll
gash your eyes!
LE.   Despite you—
DA.   Stand! whereto?
LE.   To vulcanize Venus.
TR.   Will he knock?
LE.   *Anyone* in!
DA.   Rap'n' I'll reap your face!
1 WH.   No coals, jes' dried figs.
DA.   Coals to flame your head!
LE.   I'll look elsewhere.
DA.   Then what!
LE.   Make a fire!
DA.   Of inhumanity?
LE.   Burn both altar girls alive.

216

DA.   I'll rip your beard and
singe you into buzzard's roast!

(*Voice off—Dads'*)
          Thinking it over this is
          the monkey molested the swallows
          in the dream I dreamed

TR.   A favor, senator. Watch them
while I get my friend.
DA.   Go: come back.
TR.   Watch!
DA.   I'll
see he won't touch them!
TR.   Take care.
DA.   I'll be alright.
TR.   Mind he doesn't run off.
We've staked the hangman two
grand for *corpus delicti.*
DA.   Run!
I'm *alright.*
TR.   I'll be back!

III 5

Dads, Leno, Whips, (Polly, Amabel)

DA.   Do you, Leno, choose your
quietus, or to rest quiet?
LE.   I'm not listening, old man.
Despite you, Venus, Jove I'll
drag my girls b'their hair!
DA.   Try now!
LE.   I will!
DA.   Do!
LE.   Tell those bucks to withdraw.
DA.   Draw up!
LE.   No, they can't!
DA.   If they can?

LE.   I'll recéss.
Old man, if I grab
you in town I'm not
Leno if you smuggle off.
DA.   By all means! Meanwhile dare
touch them you'll get yours.
LE.   Hard?
DA.   A Leno's hard'll satisfy?
LE.   You don't fluster me. I'll
drag'em while you say *rape*.
DA. Do!
LE.   I will!
DA.   You *will*!
Do. Turbalio! scat! get two
clubs!
LE.   Clubs?
DA.   Proper ones! Quick!—
Today's your reception for rank!
LE.   Whew! my headgear blown with
my ship would be handy!
Salty: lemme call my girls?
DA.   Not licit! Ho! Admiral Clobber!
LE.   A pool! Tinkling—my ears!
DA.   Come take a club, Sparax!
Go stand that, *you* this
side of him—so! *Tension*!
If he touches those girls
with even a finger and
you don't send him, both
of you die. If he
quips you answer for them.
Should he lunge, break his
shins for what you're worth.
LE.   Won't they let me escape?
DA.   I've said. And when that
boy brings back his friend
race straight home. Diligence! 'Bye.
LE.   Hercules, how quickly this Fane
alters, once Venus', now Hercules'—
ancient with two club-armed statues.

Nowhere to run from Hercules,
savage seas marring earth. Polly?
1 WH.   What is it, dear?
LE.   Pox!
That wasn't my Polly speaking.
Awsh—Amabel?
2 WH.   Watch it, dear.
LE.   Trustful brutes giving human advice.
Have a heart boys—who'll
molest them?
WH.   Nor *will* we.
LE.   Me?
WH.   Not if you're careful.
LE.   Of what?
WH.   Some crashing misfortune.
LE.   Hercules, spare me!
WH.   Spare us!
LE.   O thanks, may I go!
Uh—you mean stand?
WH.   Exactly.
LE.   O deep pool of providence
today I'll conquer by standing.

(*Voice off*)

        Where is Scape,
        punning butcher
        tongue wag
        neighbor of my
        young year?
        out of the running
        asleep reads scripture
        horse with
        a curb: to circle
        is not to square.

        Study be quicked
        stalk or
        scapegoat, chatter
        of myth some
        learnèd center—

dropped from the action
Leno's still to
work out—
pimp, Misery! to circle
is not *too* square.

Not running more
Dad's man
lion not
bound to roar,
cat at
that pitch what was
he running for—
bush not
real blossom? to circle
does not square off.

Plautus: no science.
Ladies look and
be seen.
By this good light
fresh horses, to circle
is not to square.

III 6

Placey, Track, Leno, Chum, Whips (Polly, Amabel)

PL.   Mine! and Leno'd violate, tear
her from Venus's altar!
TR.   Indeed!
PL.   Couldn't you kill'im!
TR.   No sword.
PL.   No stick! stones?
TR.   Think I'd
quash a human dog with stones?
LE.   Hush it's up, Placey's come—
scraped together after I'm pulverized!
PL.   Were they sitting, Track, when
you left here.

TR.   As now.
PL.   Who preserves them?
TR.   An old
man, Venus's neighbor, firmly dedicated
served by servants. *I* managed.
PL.   Dock me Leno—right now!
LE.   Son—
PL.   *Son* me no more!
Rope for collar—broken neck:
opt while alive!
LE.   I'm neutral.
PL.   Hop down the beach, Track,
hustle our dumb witnesses to
this pimp's hanging—I'll meet
them at the town wharf—
rush back here, keep watch!
We're going, hunky, to court!
LE.   Why?
PL.   Dare ask after robbing
me, attempting abduction!
LE.   Not so.
PL.   No?!
LE.   Poor provocation, worse *qui vive*.
Anyway, I said I'd be
here, am I not here?
PL.   Tell the court! Get going
LE.   Sacred cow this rope's strangling
me—Chum!
CH.   Anyone calling me?
LE.   *This* is rape!
CH.   Lovely scene!
LE.   Won't you sub—vent it!
CH.   Who's this lassoed you?
LE.   Placey.
CH.   Now you have it! Better
repair to jail, crawling soulfully.
You've what great numbers opt.
LE.   What's that?
CH.   What they desire.
LE.   Come with me.

CH.   How persuasive.
Crawling, so Chum crawl after.
Still retentive?
LE.   I'll die!
PL.   Do,
worm! My Polly and Amabel
wait here until I return.
WH. It's safer home with us.
PL.   Please yes, thanks.
LE.   Robbers!
WH.   Rope!
LE.   Rescue me, Polly!
PL.   Squirming carcass!
LE.   Friend, save—
CH.   I repudiate friendship.
LE.   So: friendship spurns?
CH.   One *ship's* plenty.
LE.   Be damned.
CH.   Returns to you!—
All in *all*: men turn
animal: pimp worried into columbine:
pigeonhole ring round his neck:
day with his nest congregate.
I'll move on—his advocate
till my efforts jail him.

(*Voice off*)
A concept of culture joyed
a ladybird luffing the name
of the dead nothing else:
*for no man is so
watchful he never falls asleep.*
Dreams guard sleep, eyelids motion
sometimes *reason's monsters*, or
a dream unexplained *like an
unopened letter*. Scape as the
life escaped.

The pimp's friend disappears tho
the pimp remains, travelling exhumer

if corpses are willing, sensing
their *fate's up to mutation:*
the world wails: a tip
flood, mad girls dipping snuff,
the child in the morris—
there cannot be too much
music R—O—T—E
rote, fiddle

like noise of surf, the
rider counts the horse's will
to be ridden, the horse
races, compelled freedom. This is
the silent treatment: seal you
ever, leave their self-respect to
their minds, the stigma they'd
pierce'll not violate your mind—
people's words: a choice to
be made.

Their virtue's excess is vice.
A child said to father
or totem: you're a horse.
An old toothless walks: gap,
drivel, gab—diagnosed muscular and
skeletal aches, says: gadgets—I
look but don't want 'em,
tho I do not *demand*
this blossom now scent, bring
back another.

The moon washes all the
air: crescent, dear, come out
for all of us. Of
the God in the table:
that you cannot make it
eat grass. 'Signed and *dayed.*'
Dated? No not an erratum—
a felicity.

Dads

I feel happy having helped
these girls, the cleanest pair
and youngest skittish sweet you'll
find: my wife watches madly
catches me peering at them.
Sad.—What's Greave our fisherman
caught this night just past
at sea—better've stood home.
My! while that sea operates
only tempest's in his nets.
Today's catch's cooked, slipped these
fingers, fluke vehement sea mar.
My wife's crowing's prandial. *Ready!*
Prattle, my ears, vain eloquence.

IV 2

Greave

Neptune O thanks gracious patron
who salts the fishes succulence,
from whom enriched I've sped
safe with my fishing smack—
new catch thru storm comforted.
Miracle's incredible fishing, not one
ounce fish—*this* right here!
Now when night resurrected me
lucre proposed no soporific quiet:
tempest soughs, spirit risks spitting—
pauper I'm for master, serving
myself—I didn't park carcass.
Sloth piques me: lazy louts,
vigilant man rises on time,
doesn't expect master'll push for'im!
Loves' sleep—no lucre; trouble.
Me I'm no lazy pig—

now I'll afford it big,
see what I've raised sea-fishing!
Whatever's in it's heavy: gold
no man else's conscious of!
The occasion, Greave, opts freedom.
Self-counsel counsels: approach master astutely,
politically proffer hard capital for
freedom; freed, run a slavefarm,
merchant fleet—richer than everybody!
Yachting! amusements! Imitate Alexander's stringplayer,
tour everywhere the noblest celebrity,
found the great city Greavetown—
my fame's monument my reign.
Great brain store this wicker!
Lunch: salt, wine, no pickle.

(*Voice off, as Greave ropes and drags wicker*)
       As rope braided
       rude deigns, not
       to hang by,
       to tug and
       bind: no sense
       complaining: grammar's double
       negative: take reverie
       for faith *nor*
       ask thine oath:
       his story triumph
       regret blood shed:
       no need for
       the old chief
       to read or
       write, children do
       that as stars
       throb night—sky—
       the occasional songs
       also always future,
       grace their opposite—
       lovable awkwardness: Gregor's
       story, the convict's
       wistfulness 'I'm sorry

for the children
they've no sense:'
so life writes
out the desirability
felt, perceived not
one's own: gift
of an if
that trembles a
disorder, conceives order:
safe wording what
is it to
say *I meant:*
no wish should
hurt, Job watched
weather to wish
alike all *Noël:*
friends hard to
hold, leaves' sway
on fall's branch
all colors remembered
delight the ground
tho 't blows. Like:
the river Epirus
puts out the
torch, lights it:
and the drafts
hurt: all fishermen
transfigured: cuttlefish casts
a long gut
out of her
throat: a certain
age hermit crab
occupies empty shell,
studying a wind—
discerning spared injuries:
for *their* discourse
seems to be
music: while turtledoves
silently marry, the
survivor scorning to

outlive the mate:
Red! hyacinth: Yellow!
daffodil: thatch, look
in that meadow!
water pools, see
all busy, dogs
and men, men
and dogs, everybody's
business is nobody's
(take it at
different times should
be or shouldn't.)
Lavender in window
will at first
shadow of your
rod sink if
but a bird
fly over chub,
o least shadow,
but will rise
to the top
again lie soaring
till a shadow
affright it again:
bee breeding in
long grass, found
by the mower
of it: frog,
mouth shut up
end of August:
brandling in the
bark of tanners.
And be still
moving a fly
upon the water
you yourself being
also always moving
down stream—caterpillars
moving not unlike
waves of the

sea. Of the
fire the fly
Pyrausta without the
fire we die.
No trout is
lost, no man
can lose what
e never had:
what interest our
angles pay us
lending them to
the trout, lent
him indeed for
our profit and
for his destruction.
Blustering day, waters
so troubled a
live fly cannot
be seen or
rest upon them—
human bait body
of black wool
lapt in herl
of a peacock's
tail, blue feathers
in head, or
black wool in
yellow silk: with
Summersault of the
salmon to spawn
in fresh waters:
belly's no ears
hunger upon it.
In the morning
about three or
four of the
clock, visit the
water-side   not
too near, a
little red worm

on the point
of the hook,
warmed by the
eyes more than
the sun—the
strongest swifts of
the water, caught:
glad with a
dry house overhead:
much of roots
of the grass
for there crows
follow the plough
very close, and
when the gentles
stir but as
free from frost,
and the house
of small husks,
gravel, slime, not
made by men:
to be best
that must do
it. O young
anglers we are
now where I
first met you,
a good top
is worth preserving,
choose clearest hair
of an equal
bigness, for such
break together, not
singly, and every
misery missed is
their new mercy.
Like: Diogenes at
the fair's finnimbruns—
'admiring in animals
what we hate

in men?'
A pretty poetry
to suit the
sound to the
corrupt: none legislated
into blessedness: Blest
against obstinacy: not
your envy for
my sake. Two-
year-old all wonder
ai-yi yi-yi what
apples: no book
in the country
no lecture for
love of quietness:
smokes shower: sit
close: rains May
butter—prophecy: harp

IV 3

Track, Greave

TR. Hey! yours, man!
GR.   What, man?
TR. *I'll* pull your rope!
GR.   No!
TR. A helping hand won't hurt.
GR. Terrible night, no catch, boy—
wet—not one squamous fish.
TR. Who expects fish? Let's sermonize!
GR. In any case, no!
TR.   I
won't let go!
GR.   Let go!
TR. O dear!
GR.   No! dear.
TR.   P..sss..t!
GR. Talk!

TR.   It's a pretty tale.
GR.   Tell it.
TR.   's anyone behind us?
GR.   What've I to do with
it?
TR.   Say you'll be wise!
GR.   About what? Talk!
TR.   I'll talk
if you'll shut up. Mum?
GR.   Dumb, man, yes!
TR.   O dear!
Furtively a thief made off,
I know what he made
off with: "thief, split halves
with me," I said "and
I won't spill the beans."
Thief hasn't responded. What should
he give *me?* Say *half.*
GR.   Hercules' more ample! more'n that!
Otherwise expose him!
TR.   Nice counsel!
Now cavort, it's you!
GR.   No?!
TR.   I've known that wicker's owner—
GR.   Which?!
TR.   And its perils!
GR.   I
know *those!* Lost or found:
that's neither here nor there—
whom you know or I.
It's mine beyond your hopes.
TR.   Not if th'owner—
GR.   Owner? Fretting—
not *me* who fished't up!
TR.   Neat-eh?
GR.   The sea owns fish,
my catch is my own—
no other hand's least right
to sell for a living,
surely the sea is commonage.

231

TR.   Right! then that wicker's *ours*
invested with the cómmunal sea.
GR.   Impudence! your memorial of the
law would bury all fishermen.
Quick as they could market
none would buy, everybody push
dickering over a common share.
TR.   Who says *impudence*! Is wicker
fish? Are they the same?
GR.   Not for me to say—
hook hooks, net catches, and
whatever's caught I keep myself.
TR.   Hercules! not if it *contains*.
GR.   Philosopher!
TR.   Look, venom! has any
fisher caught, produced a wicker-fish?
You've no monopoly of occupations
wicker-worker and fisher, passel pustule!
Best demonstrate your wicker-fish or
unhand neither seaborn nor squamous.
GR.   Wha-at! not heard o'wicker-fish?!
TR.   Rascal!
GR.   I fish, I know!
Rare to catch, few land.
TR.   Little I care, ya fourflusher.
GR.   Little passel, nearly *that* color:
big, Punic-red—my item; others
black.
TR.   Exactly! Watch! twice-converted wicker-fish
it'll turn Punic-red, then black
whipped naked.
GR.   Bloody well am—
TR.   Wasting words, time. Do you
know a judge who'll arbitrate?
GR.   Wicker, arbitrate! Do true!
TR.   Stupid!
GR.   Thales!
TR.   Let go' this thing!
Let arbitrator arbitrate!
GR.   You sane?

232

TR.   Hellbent on't!
GR.   I'm crazy, mind
made up. *No!*
TR.   Say *No*—
I'll strew your brains! Le'go-o!
or I'll wring the dripping
ooze out of that thing!
GR.   Touch me you're squashed polypus!
Fight?!
TR.   Fuss? Let's just divvy.
GR.   No fruits but trouble, pustule—
I'm going home.
TR.   I've roped
you! dock ya now!
GR.   I'm helmsman
drop the rope!
TR.   Wicker first!
GR.   Today Hercules can't ram me!
TR.   Don't deny me or sequester
the wicker to a go-between.
GR.   What! the wicker I fished?
TR.   —when I peeped on shore—
GR.   My work, net, and dory?
TR.   But I peeked: to the
owner I stole like you.
GR.   Legally!
TR.   Come again—I share
the blame and not the goods?!
GR.   I don't know your urban
laws: *it's mine.*
TR.   Yea *mine*!
GR.   Man! thinking't over you're neither
thief nor accomplice.
TR.   What now?
GR.   Let me be; go and—
quiet! Don't say anything, I'll
give you nothing. Fair enough?
TR.   Haw-kid! any other conditions?
GR.   I've made'm. Le'go the rope.
TR.   Man, I'll condition you!

GR.   Hercules!
take off.
TR.   Know anybody around?
GR.   My neighbors.
TR.   Where's your place?
GR.   O-o-off there in these meadows.
TR.   Let the man lives *there*
arbitrate?
GR.   Stop pulling—le'me think.
TR.   *Fiat!*

(*Voice off—Greave's*)
                 Gee! *mine* in perpetuity:
Offering master's house! Master'll judge.
He'll see to his own.
That innocent! Bet I'll arbitrate.

TR.   Settled?
GR.   I'm certain it's mine,
but we'll not fight—*yes*.
TR.   That's talking!
GR.   If your arbitrator's
square I'll know him tho
I don't—otherwise I won't.

(*Voice off*)
                 Now disallow legal make-believe
                 sabotage down the road
                 vest price, wage and
                 right, aliens of uneasy
                 feet in delay: mastheads
                 profound and alert, usufruct
                 sage, living not quite:
                 price, wage and right
                 lumped—humped as wrongs.

Dads, Polly, Amabel, Greave, Track (Whips)

DA.   Terribly sorry, dears, I'd shelter
you, but my wife'd throw
me out, call you whores.
The altar's safer—for *you*.
PO. & AM.   We'll die.
DA.   Don't—you're safe.
No one will hurt them—
go in, Whips! I'm here.
GR.   Mornin', governor!
DA.   Greave!
TR.   Your man?
GR.   Unreputed!
TR.   Not talkin' to you!
GR.   So go!
TR.   Your man, senator?
DA.   Yes.
TR.   Greetings—again!
DA.   -   Hello! back
from your friend?
TR.   And recognized!
DA.   What's new?
TR.   He's—your man?
DA.   Yes.
TR.   Glory be!
DA.   Negotiating again?
TR.   *This* rascal!
DA.   What's he done?
TR.   I'd string'im by th'heels!
DA.   Why the row?
TR.   I'll explain.
GR.   No I'll—
TR.   I began.
GR.   Shame
should make you quit!

DA.   Quiet
Greave!
GR.   And let him peach?!
DA.   You'll wait your turn.
GR.   You'll
hear th'alien preach first?
TR.   Incompressible!
—Senator, that Leno you thrust
from the Fane—this clown
made off with *his* wicker.
GR.   Not *made off*!
TR.   Deny I'm
looking at it.
GR.   Go blind!
Have, haven't—keep away, nosey!
TR.   Is it yours honestly?
GR.   Honest—
mine or hang me, dragged
in my net—how yours?
TR.   Liar! It's as *I* say!
GR.   Why!
TR.   Senator, shut him up!
GR.   Dads doesn't abuse us as
your boss does you!
DA.   Greave,
he talks sense—his turn!
TR.   I've no claim to that
wicker, but it contains a
little jewelbox legally this girl's—
DA.   my compatriot, you said before?
TR.   I did. Her baby charms
are in it, of no
use to him, may help
find her parents.
DA.   He'll do it.
GR.   Hell I will!
TR.   *Only* the
jewelbox and charms!
GR.   Maybe they're
gold.

TR.   Means so much? You'll
be repaid in kind.
GR.   Show
gold, you'll see the jewelbox.
DA.   Keep still, Greave—resume, *you*.
TR.   O sir feel for her,
it may be Leno's wicker—
my hunch, only a feeling.
GR.   See the louse's springe?
TR.   I'm
saying if the wicker's Leno's
the girls'll know it, let
them look.
GR.   Let them look?!
DA.   It's no inequity to show
them—Greave—
GR.   I'll say inequity!
DA.   Why?
GR.   They'll jump *it's his*!
TR.   Liar! is everybody perjured noddle?
GR.   Whatever patter master backs *me*!
TR.   Maybe—but he'll hear *me*!
DA.   Greave, turn off—*you*, expedite.
TR.   Wasn't I clear? I'll repeat:
These girls are not menials—
Polly a kidnapped Athenian baby.
GR.   Menial—kidnapped—are they wicker?
TR.   Your mind, rascal, defies daylight.
DA.   Stint maledictions, prorogue to divulge!
TR.   Likely the wicker holds a
jewelbox of rush with baby
charms in it proving Athenian
parents—I've said that before.
GR.   Croak! can't the girls talk?
TR.   Nice girls do better quiet.
GR.   Seems your sex's fifty-fifty.
TR.   What!
GR.   When do *I* talk?
DA.   Do
I'll break your head!

237

TR.   Senator
make him hand over the
jewelbox, he'll be rewarded and
can keep the wicker.
GR.   So
it's mine tho you wanted
half!
TR.   That'll come later!
GR.   Hawks
sometimes gape for nothing!
DA.   Dumb!
GR.   If he's dumb first!
DA.   Greave,
hand over that wicker!
GR.   Alright
look, but I want it
back!
DA.   You'll get it back.
GR.   Here!
DA.   Polly, Amabel, listen both!
Do you recognize this?
PO.   Yes!
GR.   Misery! it's plain *yes* before
she looks.
PO.   Let me explain,
likely the wicker holds a
jewelbox of rush, I'll itemize
what's in it without looking:
if it isn't there I
lose, then everything is yours —
if true, *please* return it
to me.
DA.   That's fair enough.
GR.   It's unfair! What if she's
a harlotguessing wonder, ought she
to have it?
DA.   It will
have to be true: wonderworking
won't help, *I* look *first*!
GR.   Here goes, the rope's off!

238

DA.   A jewelbox—is this th'one?
PO.   This! o my parents here
as I hoped for you!
GR.   God help you—in *that*
box, stingy, you're squeezing them!
DA.   Greave, check here. Girl, from
way off, verify all you
recall, miss one trifle there'll
be no turns around later.
GR.   That's justice!
TR.   Hardly your type.
DA.   Talk girl—Greave, keep still.
PO.   There are charms—
DA.   Yes!
TR.   Gong!
don't show them!
DA.   Looking like—
PO.   A gold little sword with
letters on't.
DA.   What letters?
PO.   My
father's name. Somewhere not far
a tiny two-edged axe, also
gold with my mother's name.
DA.   Name—what name's on the
sword—your father's name—
PO.   Dads.
DA.   God, is this my hope?
GR.   What about *me!*
TR.   God—proceed!
GR.   Now easy you—or croak!
DA.   Your mother's name now—
PO.   Dadsallhis.
DA.   God you've served my wish!
GR.   I'm curst!
DA.   She's my daughter, Greave.
GR.   What's she t'me! Be curst
who spied me and me
fooled dragging my net from
the sea!

239

PO.   —a little silver sickle, two
little clasped hands, a little
sow—
GR.   Drat you, sow and
attachments!
PO.   —a gold charm my father
gave me for my birthday—
DA.   O pérfect! I embrace you,
greetings, my daughter, I'm Dads
your own father, saw you
born, Dadsallhis your mother's indoors!
PO.   Father I never expected!
DA.   Blessings,
beloved.
TR.   Walloping rewards for piety!
DA.   Can you make it, Track,
with the wicker inside?
TR.   Poor
Greave—no luck at all!
DA.   Come, my daughter, your mother
must confirm us, knowing more.
TR.   Come, together as we've come!
PO.   Come, Amabel.
AM.   God loves you, dear.
GR.   Peed slantwise fishing that wicker—
fished not to seclude it—
dreamed life coming to me
come alive from that sea—
crave: gold, silver's in it—
better go in, hang myself?
salt despair, slake my grief.

(*Voice off*)
        I cannot submit to the loss of the *salarium* ..
        greater care must be taken satisfying the modern *gustum* ..

        "Georg Erdmann:
        I am subjected to annoyance, jealousy and persecution.
        If your Honour knows or should hear of
        a *convenable station* .. L's a healthy place .. for the

240

past year I have received about 100 less than
usual in funeral *accidentia* .. The cost of living
so *excessive* .. *all musici* .. from my own *familie,*
I assure you I can arrange a concert *vocaliter* and
instrumentaliter .. I should trespass .. on your
forbearance were I to *incommode*
your Honour further.

Bach"

IV 5

Dads

Prodigal immortals who is more
fortunate—providentially finding my daughter.
When gods bless they do
covenant with our pious wishes.
Who in himself finds credence?
It's providentially I've found her,
to marry her to a
noble lad, my Athenian relative
who should hurry here soon:
his friend's to bring him
from the forum. What's happening
to my orders—and indoors?
Wonders! My wife's arms still
clasp daughter's neck—almost silly.

IV 6

Dads, Track

DA.   Time you stopped dandling, mother,
do some chores for my
prayers for our growing family!
Sacral lamb, pig! Don't stall
Track, whoobsx here he is!
TR.   I'll hunt up Placey, Polly!
DA.   Tell him about my daughter,
urge him t'come *now*!
TR.   Likely!

DA. Confirm he'll marry her!
TR.   Likely!
DA. That his pa's my relative!
TR. Likely!
DA.   Hurry!
TR.   Likely!
DA.   Dinner's waiting!
TR. Likely!
DA.   Everything's likely?
TR.   Likely! But
remember you promised me—
DA.   likely!
TR.   —that Placey'll grant my manumission!
DA. Likely!
TR.   Polly's word would facilitate!
DA. Likely!
TR.   Amabel's mine promptly!
DA.   Likely!
TR. You'll assure my reward!
DA.   Likely!
TR. Everything's *likely?*
DA.   *Likely* for *likely!*
Hurry boy, hurry back!
TR.   Likely!
Meanwhile you work for me!
DA. Likely!—Rascal! likely he's likely!
My ears—ho!—his *likely*!

IV 7

Greave, Dads

(*Voice off*)

            Bed joy and prosperity
            in a public situation
            we must all be immortal
            or none

            as what wind blood
            the young what journey

242

warm   that let be
may be

bubble breathes its colors
flyweight *intuition* better *look upon
guard risk* a respond to
talk to

panther's screams   feared night
bears preyed on the swine
born for common meadow
dads *cultus*

died for common meadow
forborne by "commonwealth"   said
some didn't live the quotes
in between

sons daughters not wild
as made and wild
as come   soldiering returned
unpaid scars

philosophers A Golden Age
when their need was least
brains diverse as palates
imaginary missionaries

once She now Eunuch
reigned   something new   one man
inadequate to so great
a load

but did they need
an altar to flatter
his persecutor or imitate
the victim

A blind date with
principle old shoes the profit
a bridge waiting the
river crossed

perfection understanding's satisfaction invariably
from not being able
to leave undone what
is doing

a fable a roped bull
one thing to till
by right another for
one's life

like control's rhythmic onwardness
desirable is rarely computed
no assent above conviction
gentleness courtesy

tho institutes cultivate to
restrain   sure's foolishness to
deprive another of numbers one
lacks   lack's

where man claims his soil
what to it adheres
he cannot carry where
he please

shadowboxing horse sound of
skin and skeleton free from
faults and faculties with
the arguments

he dare not admit
and yet cannot deny—
Attained south wing five windows
caged singing

ribbon of river evangelist-
scraping roofs yellow fronts
sleepless in a city
of thieves

who cannot foretell evening
from morning   trafficked streets
still cobbled   Could be
a sphere

of pyramidal honeycomb, the
sphere enclosing the most space
with the least surface
strongest against

internal pressure   the honeys
enclosing the least space   most
surface best to withstand
external pressures

could be one lean buck
take heart grow fuller
knowing like transported cargo
smells of

portage the winter-wrapped tree
elsewhere May   a summer's
dory unstowed so much
so little

each one's house just
float off   nations just stops
and wander that needs
no feet

                    begin
                    anywhere

GR.   When's't likely we'll talk, Dads?
DA.   Negotiating, Greave?
GR.   That old wicker—
be wise, keep God's gift.
DA.   Can another's possessions be mine?
GR.   My bread from the sea?
DA.   He's fortunate who lost it,
still the wicker isn't yours.

GR.   Always the saintly pious pauper!
DA.   O Greave, Greave, a man
is lured into deception, snares
a hell of poisoned bait:
whoever's avid for this is
trapped in his own avarice.
But if he consults deeply
he lives longer by honesty.
That greedy wicker'll prey more
on us than it's worth.
How can I hide it—
it's another's! *Not our Dads!*
Wise men'll never share the
conscience of slaves in crime.
I don't care for lucre.
GR.   I've experienced comedians declaiming wisdom
applauded by the audience out
there—they're called people—everybody
so divorced going home all
information about rectitude proves useless.
DA.   Go, nag! Temper your tongue.
You'll get nothing, just frustrations.
GR.   Good—God! change all good
in that wicker to cinders.

DA.   You've looked at our servants.
Had he found an accomplice
both'd be stringing out lives
as crooks: lout looting soul,
crony preyed on by loot.
Better to sacrifice: give thanks
and see our dinner's cooking.

IV 8

Placey, Track

PL.   Ditto my love, my Track
my libertine, sponsor, almost father—
Polly's uncovered her folks?
TR.   Ditto.
PL.   *My country-folk?*

TR.   Opine.

PL.   We'll marry?

TR.   Suspected.

PL.   Dads consents today?

TR.   Consent-ho!

PL.   Congratulations to her father?

TR.   Consent-ho!

PL.   Her mother?

TR.   Consent-ho!

PL.   What's consented?

TR.   *What's* consented!

PL.   In what sense?

TR.   I consent-ho!

PL.   How many senses?

TR.   *Me* consent-ho!

PL.   As I'm here
consent ever?

TR.   Consent-ho!

PL.   Shall I
run?

TR.   Consent-ho!

PL.   Or look poised?

TR.   Consent-ho!

PL.   Salute her coming?

TR.   Consent-ho!

PL.   And her father?

TR.   Consent-ho!

PL.   And her
mother?

TR.   Consent-ho!

PL.   Embrace father?

TR.   Oh-no!

PL.   Embrace mother?

TR.   Oh-no!

PL   Kiss my—
girl?

TR.   Oh-no!

PL.   No consent-ho?!

TR.   Nuts let's go!

PL.   Tuck my sponsor.

247

Leno

Whose misery beats mine, now
Placey's judges have condemned me?
Polly's adjudicated free, perdition's mine.
Lenos! Joy procreates pimps so
the world enjoys their downfall.
Amabel's in Venus Fane—I
must have'r! my last relic!

(*Voice off*)
        When Plautus lay dead Comedy wept
        an empty scene, laughs, lewd mimes, jokes hushed,
        innumerable simultaneous numbers clamoring around
        Tragedy voicing the dead smile undivined good—

        Old friends
        when I was young
        you laughed with my tongue
        but when I sang
        for forty years
        you hid in your ears
        hardly a greeting

        I was
        being poor
        termed difficult
        tho I attracted a cult
        of leeches
        and they signed *love*
        and drank its cordials
        always for giving
        when they were receiving
        they presumed
        an infinite forgiveness

        With my weak eyes
        I did not see

assumed a bit
of infinite myself
arrogating hypocrisy
to *no* heart
but stupidity

O it was
better better
than equating favors
a few to my balance
years later
charged as
cantankerous
in their senile scrounging
getting on

And tho love starve
carved mostly bones
(not *those* young friends
put to good use)
if I'm not dead
a dead mask smiles
to all old friends
still young where else
it says *take care*
prosper
without my tongue
only your own

V 2

Greave, Leno

GR.   Spiteful men! Vesper won't bring
back Greave without his wicker.

(*Voice off—Leno's*)
        O that word *wicker* hurts!

GR.   That scut Track's free and
I who worked get nothing.

(Voice off—Leno nearer)
>   Prodigal immortals an arresting summons!

GR.   God! I'll placard th'dump, big
letters! LOST WICKER TREASURES—FOUND
GREAVE: don't presume it's yours!

(Voice off—Leno hurrying)
>   Hercules' probably my wicker I
>   must ask—o gods subvene!

GR.   Who wants me indoors? I'm
polishing. God, rust not iron,
the more it's polished 'treddens
thinner, consumes in my hands.
LE.   Howdy, boy!
GR.   Bless old curls!
LE.   Whatya doin?
GR.   Polishing.
LE.   Feel alright?
GR.   Medic?
LE.   A letter longer—
GR.   Pauper!
LE.   That's cute!
GR.   Not your face!
LE.   That's its misery last night's
shipwreck leaves, washed-up nothing.
GR.   All
departed?
LE.   A wickerful of treasure.
GR.   Can you itemize?
LE.   What good
is that? Fable says more.
GR.   If found—some token—proof?
LE.   Eight hundred Philips marsupially wrapped,
one sack assorted Tetrarch Philips!

(Voice off—Greave's)
>   Hercules' load concupiscence the Gods
>   respect men! o I can
>   prey on his wicker

GR.   And—
LE.   Silver: one grand—nothing crummy!
bowl, tankard, pitcher, jug, ladle.
GR.   Pap you had it luscious!
LE.   *Had's* misery's *not to have.*
GR.   What will you give to
have it back?
LE.   Thirty—
GR.   Tripes!
LE.   Forty smackers!
GR.   Peanuts!
LE.   Fifty.
GR.   Dental floss!
LE.   Sixty.
GR.   Bugs in rugs.
LE.   How about seventy!
GR.   Hot refrigerants.
LE.   One hundred—
GR.   asleep?
LE.   That's *top.*
GR.   S'long.
LE.   Once I go I go—one-ten?
GR.   Doormice.
LE.   How much then, pustule?
GR.   Two grand: more? not less.
Yes'r no?
LE.   What choice's necessity?
Settled.
GR.   Addréss Venus!
LE.   Love's pleasure's
imperative.
GR.   Touch her altar.
LE.   Touch'n'go!
GR.   Swear!
LE.   *Swear, man?!*
GR.   Repeat!
LE.   Say!

(*Voice off—Leno's*)
          Dumb—been swearin' all along!

251

GR.   Hand there?

LE.   Holding!

GR.   Reward due
once the wicker's yours—

LE.   Right!

GR. (& LE.) *Cyrenian Venus attest my testimony*
if my wicker sunk in
your sea with all in
it come back to me
Greave here—now touch me

LE.   *Greave here*—hear me Venus—
receives two grand immediately!

GR.   Add, if fraud tempts you
may Venus destroy your sort—

(*Voice off—Greave's*)
           But curse you either way!

LE.   If I trick him, Venus,
then see all pimps destroyed!

(*Voice off—Greave's*)
           That must be tho you
           swear true—

GR.   Let me get
Dads to hear your claim.

LE.   If that grouch procures my
wicker I owe him nothing.
I arbitrate despite tongue swearing.
Continence! he comes with senility.

(*Voice off—Leno's*)
           O beautiful horrors I've suffered
           the law's not for Grouch!

Greave, Dads, Leno

GR. Come, come Dads.

DA.   Where's Leno?

GR. Hey! Here's Dads—has it!

DA. Yes, if it's yours you'll
have it. Sound! Take it!

LE. Prodigal imortals w .. wu .. wicker, wicker!

DA. Yours?

LE.   Don't ask! Mine b'Jove!

DA. Intact—less a jewelbox of
baby charms identifying my daughter.

LE. How!

DA.   Your Polly's my daughter.

LE. Glad you made it!

DA.   Like
incredible?

LE.   No I'm delighted! I
condone her—take her gratis.

DA. Thank you!

LE.   Man, *thank you*!

GR. Not so fast, Mr Wicker!

LE. Fast?

GR.   Cash! my two grand!

LE. What bloody nonsense!

GR.   Nonsense? Don't
you owe me—

LE.   Hell no!

GR. Didn't you swear?

LE.   Swearing's voluptuous—
pleasure's my hoard, property's no
condominium.

GR.   Two grand! You perjurer!

DA. Greave, what's this two grand?

GR. He swore—promised me!

LE.   I
like to swear—objéct, Pontifex?

DA. Why did he promise, Greave?

GR.   He swore if I got
the wicker back to him
he'd pay two grand.
LE.   Let
someone responsible settle this quickly
he cóntracted to axe me—
and me not of age!
GR.   Dads is *someone*!
LE.   *Anybody* else!

(*Voice off—Dads'*)
                I cannot rob Greave if
                I condemn the pimp—

DA.   Leno!
Did you promise him money?
LE.   I did.
DA.   What you promised
my help is mine. Pimp—
it's no use.
GR.   Thought you'd
rat, pimp! Hand it over!
I'll give it to Dads,
be free on my own.
DA.   I gave you, Leno, what
I salvaged—
GR.   No! I! I!
DA.   If *you're* wise keep quiet—
Leno, do I deserve a
favor?
LE.   Having implied my rights—
DA.   Rather a miracle I've not
encroached?
GR.   Leno labors: liberty's born!
DA.   This man found your wicker
and I gave it to you.
LE.   Thanks owes *you* two grand!
GR.   Owes *me*—you!
DA.   Shut up!

254

GR.   How munificence works for yourself
to rob me again as
you did of the jewelbox.
DA.   Want to be slapped?
GR.   Slap for all I care—
nothing less than two grand
will shut me up!
LE.   He's
for you idiot! Silence!
DA.   Let's
talk alone, Leno.
LE.   Let's!
GR.   Come out in the open!
DA.   Sh .. h .. what did Amabel cost?
LE.   One grand.
DA.   May I offer—
LE.   Sounds sensible.
DA.   We'll divide—
LE.   yes?
DA.   One grand yours for her,
the other for me—
LE.   good!
DA.   which—don't tell him—I'll
give Greave who found both
your wicker *and* my daughter.
LE.   Good!
GR.   When do I get mine!
DA.   Settled, Greave, I have it.
GR.   You! but *I* want it!
DA.   No-o-o, don't hope, free him
from his oath!
GR.   May I
die you'll never cheat again!
DA.   We dine today, Leno!
LE.   Obliged!
DA.   Come with me—gentlemen in
the audience I'd invite you
too, only we've no setups
and you have standing invitations.
But if you'll applaud—all

under sixteen, welcome! None?
Come then—*both*!

EPILOGUE I—GREAVE

Free. I am fain Fane
old word pun of a
fancy of a nine-year old's
Shakespeare *Fane* Plautus' Diphilus dream
jests of a tempest *Kings*
dalas poorest we had all
droll roll and gambol risk
of a playful sea   Saturday
matinee and night   and Sunday
matinee and night child in
the morris harp

LE.   O let's!

EPILOGUE II—DADS

Applaud.

(*Voice off—as the audience is already
moving out*)

Sweet   turn on your side.

(*continues*)